GOD
HIMSELF

GOD
HIMSELF

A JOURNEY THROUGH HIS ATTRIBUTES

TONY EVANS

MOODY PUBLISHERS

CHICAGO

Some content in this book is adapted from Tony Evans, *Our God Is Awesome: Encountering the Greatness of Our God* (Chicago: Moody, 1994) and Tony Evans, "God Is in Control," The Urban Alternative, https://tonyevans.org/god-is-in-control/.

All Scripture quotations, unless otherwise indicated, are taken from the New American Standard Bible®, Copyright © 1960, 1962, 1963, 1968, 1971, 1972, 1973, 1975, 1977, 1995 by The Lockman Foundation. Used by permission. (www.Lockman.org)

Scripture quotations marked NIV are taken from the Holy Bible, New International Version®, NIV®. Copyright © 1973, 1978, 1984, 2011 by Biblica, Inc.™ Used by permission of Zondervan. All rights reserved worldwide. www.zondervan.com. The "NIV" and "New International Version" are trademarks registered in the United States Patent and Trademark Office by Biblica, Inc.™

Scripture quotations marked KJV are taken from the King James Version.

Edited by Kevin P. Emmert
Interior and cover design: Erik M.Peterson
Cover photo by Gabriel Garcia Marengo on Unsplash

All websites and phone numbers listed herein are accurate at the time of publication but may change in the future or cease to exist. The listing of website references and resources does not imply publisher endorsement of the site's entire contents. Groups and organizations are listed for informational purposes, and listing does not imply publisher endorsement of their activities.

Library of Congress Cataloging-in-Publication Data

Names: Evans, Tony, 1949- author.
Title: God, himself : a journey through his attributes / Tony Evans.
Description: Chicago, IL : Moody Publishers, 2020. | Includes
  bibliographical references. | Summary: "Join Tony Evans as he dives into
  the character of our awesome God—one attribute at a time. You'll learn
  about attributes like God's wisdom and word, His sufficiency and
  sovereignty, and His goodness, grace, and glory that make Him—our
  Heavenly Father—the great God that He is"—Provided by publisher.
Identifiers: LCCN 2020015687 (print) | LCCN 2020015688 (ebook) | ISBN
  9780802418166 (paperback) | ISBN 9780802496621 (ebook)
Subjects: LCSH: God (Christianity)—Attributes.
Classification: LCC BT130 .E94 2020 (print) | LCC BT130 (ebook) | DDC
  231/.4—dc23
LC record available at https://lccn.loc.gov/2020015687
LC ebook record available at https://lccn.loc.gov/2020015688

Originally delivered by fleets of horse-drawn wagons, the affordable paperbacks from D. L. Moody's publishing house resourced the church and served everyday people. Now, after more than 125 years of publishing and ministry, Moody Publishers' mission remains the same—even if our delivery systems have changed a bit. For more information on other books (and resources) created from a biblical perspective, go to: www.moody publishers.com or write to:

Moody Publishers
820 N. LaSalle Boulevard
Chicago, IL 60610

3 5 7 9 10 8 6 4

Printed in the United States of America

CONTENTS

Chapter 1:   The Nature of God   7

Chapter 2:   The Allness of God   33

Chapter 3:   The Holiness of God   61

Chapter 4:   The Wrath of God   83

Chapter 5:   The Sovereignty of God   105

Chapter 6:   The Love of God   129

Chapter 7:   The Wisdom of God   147

Chapter 8:   The Goodness of God   167

Chapter 9:   The Grace of God   185

Chapter 10: The Glory of God   209

Appendix: The Urban Alternative   229

Acknowledgments   237

Chapter 1
_____

THE NATURE OF GOD

O nce upon a time, a scorpion needed to cross a pond. Wondering how he would get to the other side, he noticed a frog nearby. "Mr. Frog, will you please hop me across this pond?"

The kind, gentle frog said, "Certainly, Mr. Scorpion. I will be glad to do so."

So Mr. Scorpion jumped onto Mr. Frog's back as Mr. Frog hopped from pad to pad, bringing Mr. Scorpion to the other side of the pond. But just as the frog said, "Well, Mr. Scorpion, here we are," he felt an excruciating pain in his back. Mr. Scorpion had stung him.

As Mr. Frog lay dying, he looked up at Mr. Scorpion and said, "How could you do this? I brought you from one side of the pond to the other, and now you sting me so that I die."

Mr. Scorpion looked at Mr. Frog and said, "I can't help it. It's my nature."

It's important to know the nature of the one you are dealing with. If you think you are getting one thing, but when you get it, it's not what you thought it was, you could be in trouble. That happens today with a lot of errant teaching about who God is. God has been so misdefined, tragically redefined, and even dismissed that people do not understand His true nature and, as a result, get stuck with false and damaging views of God.

Had the frog taken into account the true nature of the scorpion, he would have never let him hop on his back. Our understanding of someone or something else influences our connection with and relation to the other. To misunderstand the nature of God is no small thing. Rather, our failing to know God as He truly is leads to our failure to access the abundant life Jesus Christ came to give (John 10:10). It also takes us off course from living out the purpose He has for us, as well as negatively influencing all our relationships with each other, and our love toward ourselves.

When you or I make decisions based on a misunderstanding of God's nature, thinking that we know the true God when in fact we know something totally different from who and what the true God is, the results of those decisions will lead to destruction and death. Now, that may not mean physical death, but it certainly means spiritual, relational, and even emotional death. Knowing the nature of God as He reveals Himself, rather than how we think He is, can save us from a life of confusion and defeat.

God's nature consists in His intrinsic traits. *Nature*, after all, is the inherent characteristics that define any being, animal, or thing. To study and come to know God's nature ought to be the preeminent focus and desire of all believers in Christ. This is because there is no greater knowledge that you can possess outside of the knowledge of God. To know God means you come to understand and reflect His nature. Jeremiah 9:23–24 emphasizes the importance of this pursuit:

> Thus says the LORD, "Let not a wise man boast of his wisdom, and let not the mighty man boast of his might, let not a rich man boast of his riches; but let him who boasts boast of this, that he understands and knows Me, that I am the LORD who exercises lovingkindness, justice and righteousness on earth; for I delight in these things," declares the LORD.

Wisdom, might, and riches are of no importance when placed against the backdrop of knowing God. In this passage, we are told clearly not to boast about anything other than knowing and understanding God. The knowledge of God is life's greatest pursuit. When you relegate the knowing and understanding of God to a second-rate discovery, you have unwittingly lessened your ability to know anything else at all. All truth arises from God Himself. In fact, failing to know God fully will similarly keep you from knowing yourself.

You and I were created in the image of God. We exist to be mirrors of His nature, yet in a finite manner. Thus, the better you come to know and understand God, the better you will understand yourself. As you come to recognize and see God more clearly for who He truly is, you will also discover who you are as well as understand the world around you.

IN THE BEGINNING, GOD

It's always best to start at the beginning, so that's what we are going to do in our discovery of God's nature. The very first verse in Scripture says, "In the beginning God created the heavens and the earth" (Gen. 1:1). Now, that may seem like a short verse, and when you compare it to other passages in the Bible it is a relatively short verse. But in this one introductory verse, we find a significant amount of meaning.

For starters, the Bible does not begin by trying to account for God's existence in one form or another. What we don't read is just as important as what we do. Nowhere do we find a defense argument trying to prove that God exists. Rather, Psalm 14:1 tells us that if you don't believe in God, you are a fool. It says, "The fool has said in his heart, 'There is no God.'"

So much debate goes on today about whether God even exists, yet the Bible begins on this assumption because His existence is self-evident. Nature itself attests to the existence of God, since the heavens and earth declare His glory (Ps. 19:1). The galaxies, stars, mathematical precision of all created things, and living beings proclaim God's reality. To deny God exists in light of the impossibility of the creation in which we live is foolish. Romans 1:20 states it this way:

> For since the creation of the world His invisible attributes, His eternal power and divine nature, have been clearly seen, being understood through what has been made, so that they are without excuse.

Just as you cannot have a watch without a watchmaker or a painting without a painter or a building without a builder, you also cannot have a creation without a Creator. And the cause must be sufficient to bring about the result. Whether it's a refusal to believe by the overwhelming majority of physicists and astronomers who study our universe, or whether it arises out of hearts that do not want to be held accountable, the notion that God does not exist is a notion without excuse. It is a notion based on lies and falsehoods. Scripture (and the created order) is clear that God exists. Should the earth move roughly the distance between the moon and the earth, times four either closer to or further from the sun, the earth itself would be uninhabitable. Yet it doesn't because it is held in place by Christ. Not only were all things created by Him, but He also holds them all in order. Colossians 1:16–17 states it like this:

> For by Him all things were created, both in the heavens and on earth, visible and invisible, whether thrones or dominions or rulers or authorities—all things have been created through Him and for Him. He is before all things, and in Him all things hold together.

This truth introduces our first aspect about God, which is that He is transcendent. He existed before all things and is not limited to space or time. He is totally distinct from His creation. The word *distinct* is a synonym for transcendent. God is unique. He is one of a kind. You can make no comparison that will give you an understanding of God unless He grants that comparison because there is nothing you can compare Him to.

That's the problem with coming up with your own idea of God. If it's your idea, the idea is probably wrong. The only understanding you can get of God's nature is the understanding He gives you because nothing else in the universe is like Him.

God exists above His creation. A key passage for this powerful truth is found in Isaiah 40:

To whom then will you liken God?
Or what likeness will you compare with Him?
As for the idol, a craftsman casts it,
A goldsmith plates it with gold,
And a silversmith fashions chains of silver.
He who is too impoverished for such an offering
Selects a tree that does not rot;
He seeks out for himself a skillful craftsman
To prepare an idol that will not totter.

Do you not know? Have you not heard?
Has it not been declared to you from the beginning?
Have you not understood from the foundations of the earth?
It is He who sits above the circle of the earth,
And its inhabitants are like grasshoppers,
Who stretches out the heavens like a curtain
And spreads them out like a tent to dwell in.
He it is who reduces rulers to nothing,
Who makes the judges of the earth meaningless. . . .

"To whom then will you liken Me
that I should be his equal?" says the Holy One.
Lift up your eyes on high

The Nature of God

And see who has created these stars,
The One who leads forth their host by number,
He calls them all by name;
Because of the greatness of His might and the strength
   of His power
Not one of them is missing. (vv. 18–23, 25–26)

God is the transcendently perfect, uncreated Creator, Sustainer, and Ruler of all things.. God is so spectacular in His creative power that He can take two cells that come together and turn them into billions upon billions of cells that comprise a solitary human body. Scientists have discovered that each human life consists of roughly thirty-two trillion cells. Before you can wrap your mind around that, also consider that every single second, each of us has approximately two million red blood cells die. That's every single second. All the while, during this same second, another two million red blood cells are being created. The frailty of a life form is beyond our own understanding. Only a mighty Creator can sustain life in the way we are sustained, let alone create it.

For example, when you crush a roach or an insect, you have disconnected its cells from each other. The cells are no longer interconnected with each other and so the insect no longer lives. The reason you and I live is not only that we have cells but also because our cells are interconnected. One cell talks with another cell. The nerves work with the muscles. Cells by billions interface in a perfectly harmonious manner with each other. Without this harmonious interfacing of billions upon billions of cells, you will not live well. Nothing will live apart from God's grand design. The human body is just one example. But

13

we also have trees, grass, animals, and more. For God to create the kind of living connections that He has produced is beyond our understanding. Yet, while you and I can't understand Him, He has also made Himself intimately available to us as well. He is the Great High God but also the very intimate, personal God, as we will see in our study on His attributes.

God is bigger than the sum total of His creation. He is infinite and boundless. Yet even though He is bigger than all creation, He has decided to mix it up with us on earth. While He lives outside time and space, He has chosen to hang out with us as well. He has chosen to locate Himself on earth, through the mechanism of the church (Eph. 2) as well as the creation of each one of us as the temple of God (1 Cor. 6:19–20). This God whom you and I are dealing with and learning about is way up in the third heaven, outside His creation, but He is also within His followers by the indwelling Spirit. We have been bought with a price to make His habitation possible.

As a result, the glory of God must be the passion of our lives and of our churches. Wherever God sees His glory comfortably residing, He makes Himself more available to His people. God's kingdom agenda involves the furthering of His glory on earth. It ought to be our individual and corporate mission statements. The kingdom agenda can be defined as the visible manifestation of the comprehensive rule of God over every area of life. It starts with surrender on a personal level, resulting in the spiritual fruit of love, grace, kindness, gentleness, forgiveness, and more. We are able to carry forward this agenda through our thoughts and actions when we recognize the nature of God as the Creator and Sustainer of all things.

THE ESSENCE OF GOD

God's transcendence also speaks to His essence. God is a spirit. He is non-material. This also means He is not physical, but rather, He is invisible. Thus, if you are going to get to know Him, you need to connect to Him spiritually. Physical activity alone does not connect directly to God because He exists as a spiritual being. Jesus sought to explain this to us as it is written in John 4:23–24, where He said,

> "But an hour is coming, and now is, when the true worshipers will worship the Father in spirit and truth; for such people the Father seeks to be His worshipers. God is spirit, and those who worship Him must worship in spirit and truth."

Our worship and understanding of God is limited when we seek to identify with Him purely on a physical level. That's one reason why He started out the Ten Commandments with the command that we not make a god before Him or any images of Him. We are to not create physical idols, even if we are seeking to make them as a replica of Him. Because whatever we fashion will fall short. The only known physical reflection of God is Jesus Christ. John 1:18 puts it this way: "No one has seen God at any time; the only begotten God who is in the bosom of the Father, He has explained Him." Jesus is, essentially, God's "selfie." He's a human picture of God. Jesus is the closest we will get to seeing or experiencing God on earth in a physical form. The only revelation of God in terms of full visibility is the person of Christ.

Outside of how He revealed Himself to us in Jesus, no one

has ever seen God. Moses once prayed, "show me Your glory" (Ex. 33:18). But the Bible says that God had to hide Moses "in the cleft of the rock" lest Moses see God and die (v. 22). That's why when you go to heaven, you must have a new body. This body would not make the transition into God's presence and survive.

Some people might object to this reality by saying, "Tony, wait a minute. How can you worship someone you can't see?" I can answer that question through a comparison. It is the same way you can know it's windy. Tell me, what does the wind look like? What are its component parts? How does it feel? No one can visuallly describe wind because it's invisible, even though you know it's there. You can say, "It's a windy day." Why? Because its effects are clear. Tree limbs bend, hats blow, umbrellas turn inside out. It's obvious when it's windy, not because you can see the wind, but because its effects are without question. God's existence and reality is clearly manifested in His creation (Ps. 19:1; Rom. 1:20).

You see the reality of God in what He does, not in what He looks like. So if God never blows any wind in your direction, you will not experientially know He's real. But if you are growing in your faith and He's blowing in your direction, even though you can't see Him, you will know He's all around you. God is invisible, yet His effects can be clearly seen.

If you are ever going to find the meaning of life and live it out, your spirit must be in touch with God's Spirit, regardless of circumstances. If you are not developing a spiritual relationship with God, you cannot personally come to know Him, for God is spirit.

Being connected to God, who is spirit, also means that you

are complete in Him (see Col. 2:9–10). Everything you need for everything He has called you to be and do is located in Him. Listen to what Paul says in Acts 17:24–25:

> The God who made the world and all things in it, since He is Lord of heaven and earth, does not dwell in temples made with hands; nor is He served by human hands, as though He needed anything, since He Himself gives to all people life and breath and all things.

Do you see what Paul is saying? He says that God is so comprehensive and so complete, He is self-generating. He is the source of all things. You and I are spiritually complete in Him if and when we do as Jeremiah 29:13 says: "You will seek Me and find Me when you search for Me with all your heart." The word "heart" in this verse is a symbol for the spirit. It indicates the internal consciousness of our soul and spirit. When we seek God with all of our spiritual being within us, we will find Him.

Conversely, when we seek Him according to our physical logic, thinking, or pursuits, there is no guarantee that we will find Him. Far too many people confuse church attendance with spiritual intimacy. But, unfortunately, someone can go to church every Sunday and yet never find God because the spiritual makeup of the heart must be in the search. If your body is in church but your spirit is not in it, you won't meet God. You may tap your feet to the music and clap your hands at the sermon, but you will not meet God. Due to the essence of God, He requires your full heart to connect with Him. He demands that you worship Him in spirit and in truth. He is spirit, and unless your spirit is in your worship, you will be no different twelve months from now from who you are today. Yet when your spirit connects to Him, based on the truth of His Word, you will experience life transformation and a release of His wisdom and authority both in and through you like you never could have imagined.

GOD IS A PERSONAL BEING

Now, while God is spirit in His essence, He is not unapproachable or unreachable. This is because He is also personal. We discover this truth in Exodus 3:13–15:

> Then Moses said to God, "Behold, I am going to the sons of Israel, and I will say to them, 'The God of your fathers has sent me to you.' Now they may say to me, 'What is His name?' What shall I say to them?" God said to Moses, "I AM WHO I AM"; and He said, "Thus you shall say to the sons of Israel, 'I AM has sent me to you.'" God, furthermore, said to Moses, "Thus you shall say to the sons of Israel, 'The LORD, the God of your fathers, the God of Abraham, the God of Isaac, and the God of Jacob, has sent me to you.' This is My name forever, and this is My memorial-name to all generations."

In this name that God reveals to us about Himself, we find the personal pronoun "I." Personal attributes include intellect, emotion, will, and consciousness. God has all of these, and more. In fact, Scripture talks about the mind of God. It also talks about His feelings, such as jealousy, love, joy, laughter, grief, and compassion.[1] God created each of us in His own image and, thus, we reflect these same emotions in our beings as well. One reason He has done this is so we could personally and intimately relate to Him and He could relate to us. God is not an ethereal puff of light floating around like a mist in the air. No, God is a personal being to whom relating can occur, as long as we discover how to do it on a spiritual level.

Another aspect of the personal nature of God is that He is a triune being. He is one God, existing in three coequal persons who are one in essence yet distinct in personhood. He is God the Father, God the Son, and God the Holy Spirit. Keep this in mind as you consider the Trinity. The Father is not the Son. The Son is not the Spirit. And yet they all share the same divine nature and attributes, just like a single pretzel has three holes that are distinct from one another yet they still are connected together by the same dough. Each member of the Trinity has a specific role that they play, although they are equal to one another in essence, glory, power, and honor.

Let's revisit the parameters again because it's important that we build our understanding on the foundational truth: There is only one God. Deuteronomy 6:4 affirms, "The LORD is our God, the LORD is one!" God Himself declares, "Besides Me there is no God" (Isa. 45:5). Paul says the same: "There is no God but one" (1 Cor. 8:4). There is only one true God, not the god of this or that religion. Yet, while we have only one God,

---

1. See 1 John 4:8; John 3:16; Jeremiah 31:3; Proverbs 6:16; Psalm 5:5; Exodus 20:5; Joshua 24:19; Zephaniah 3:17; Isaiah 62:5; Jeremiah 32:41; Genesis 6:6; Psalm 78:40; Psalm 2:4; Psalm 37:13; Proverbs 1:26; Psalm 135:14; Judges 2:18; Deuteronomy 32:36.

God is uniquely triune in His being, existing as the Father, the Son, and the Holy Spirit.

The Bible gives us a lot of information on this reality. First, we see the plurality of God in creation: "In the beginning God created the heavens and the earth" (Gen. 1:1). The Hebrew word for God here is *Elohim*, a plural word. Even in the first sentence of the Bible, God lets us know that He is plural even as He is singular.

He shows this in the creation of man, because in Genesis 1:26, God says, "Let *Us* make man in *Our* image" (emphasis added). But then the very next verse says, "*God* [*Elohim*, plural] created man in *His* [singular] own image" (emphasis added). The text moves freely from plural to singular and back to plural. Why? Because our one God exists in three persons.

We also get a glimpse of the Trinity in Isaiah 48:16, where the pre-incarnate Christ says, "the Lord GOD has sent Me, and His Spirit," associating God the Father with the Son and the Holy Spirit. That's why you can have Jesus on the cross saying to the Father, "why hast thou forsaken me?" (KJV). They are two different persons. The Father is not the Son; the Son is not the Spirit. But the Father is God, the Son is God, and the Spirit is God. All three are equal in essence, members of the singular Godhead while remaining distinct from each other in their personhood.

The plurality of God also appears in the descriptions of God. The Father is called God (Gal. 1:1, 3; Eph. 1:2–3). The Son is called God (John 20:28). The Holy Spirit is called God (Acts 5:3–4). In fact, in Hebrews 1:8, God the Father calls God the Son "God." This is why believers are baptized in the one, singular name of the triune God—Father, Son, and Holy Spirit (Matt. 28:19).

The Bible says all three persons of the Trinity are at work in salvation (1 Peter 1:1–2). Paul tells us in 2 Corinthians 13:14 that one member of the Trinity gives us grace, one member loves us, and another unites us in fellowship. These are not mutually exclusive ministries, of course. All three members of the Trinity are working together to sanctify us.

The Bible ascribes creation to God (Gen. 1:1), to Jesus (Col. 1:16), and to the Spirit (Gen. 1:2; Ps. 104:30). The Trinity is active in prayer (Eph. 2:18) and in the blessing of the believer (2 Thess. 2:13).

As a triune being, He is able to do something differently from every other so-called god humanity has invented over time. He exists as love. God is love. Yes, God loves. But, what's more, He literally *is* love. No other god can make that statement. Other religions can claim that the god they worship can love, but they cannot say that their god *is* love. Because in order to love or be loved, you have to have existed in a state of having somebody to love.

So the question is: Who did God love when there was nobody to love? He loved Himself, existing as the Trinity. The Godhead eternally lives in community. He exists as singular and plural at the same time. God's personal, singular nature also includes the perfect unity found in His Triune nature. All three persons of the Trinity exist in this name God revealed to Moses, "I AM THAT I AM" (KJV).

GOD IS AN ETERNAL BEING

When we dig even deeper to uncover the attributes of God revealed to us through His name "I Am That I Am," we discover that God is not only personal but also present, continually in the "now." God has eternally existed only in the present tense. He doesn't have a yesterday nor does He have a tomorrow. Time has been given to humanity for the reasons God has, in His wisdom, chosen for us. Yet when it comes to God and His attributes, He is the timeless God—forever existing in the present moment. To God, all moments are present. That's how He can know the end from the beginning (Isa. 46:10) because to God, there is no end and there is no beginning. Humanity lives in this dimension of time while God exists outside of it, not bound by it. Everything for God is "now."

We may not be able to appreciate this attribute of God as much as we should because we are linear beings. We live in a continuum known as time and space. It progresses forward in a linear, beginning-to-end path. But when we transition to our eternal reality known as paradise, heaven, we will be in that place where there is no day, no night, no sleep, and no time, as Scripture states (see Rev. 21:23). Even the concept of "time," will be meaningless once we transition to glory. God has always existed outside His creation of time while simultaneously operating in it.

I understand this is difficult to understand. In Deuteronomy 29:29, we read, "The secret things belong to the LORD our God, but the things revealed belong to us and to our sons forever, that we may observe all the words of this law." God keeps secrets. He says so in His Word. There are things that we can glimpse and seek to comprehend but will remain beyond our full awareness simply due to the differences between our nature and His.

As an eternal being, God is self-existent and self-sufficient. He doesn't need food. He doesn't need water. He doesn't need air in order to live. None of us are self-sufficient. We are dependent on many things in order to live each moment in time. But God is completely self-sufficient. His name "I Am That I Am" tells us that. It also tells us that He defines Himself. He is not defined by anyone or anything. God does not have to go outside of Himself in order to be Himself. Everything God needs is within Him. He is complete.

Nothing can be added to or taken away from God. That thought defies comprehension because we don't know anything else like that in our universe. But that explains why the Bible says nothing compares to God (Jer. 10:6).

It frustrates autonomous humans that they can't put a limit on God. They can't box Him in. The test tubes don't work when it comes to Him, nor does cloning. The mathematical formulas don't equate when it comes to God, because His sufficiency means all that makes God who He is already resides within Him.

So God does not need you or me. We need Him. God is sufficient, complete within Himself. He does not need anything in His created order to make Him feel better about being God. Job 22:2–3 says that God receives no benefit from man.

Job underscores that again by reminding us that people at their best offer nothing of benefit to God (Job 35:7–8). Jesus said that even our best, when it's placed against God, makes us "unworthy slaves" (Luke 17:10). This is true for entire nations, too: "the nations are like a drop from a bucket . . . a speck of dust on the scales" to God (Isa. 40:15). He simply blows on them, and they cease to exist.

God's self-sufficiency also means He is answerable to no one. He does not need our permission to do what He plans to do. Our complaints don't make a difference either.

What are the implications of God's sufficiency? First, you cannot help God. God will do what He is going to do no matter what you do. Therefore, He cannot be intimidated. You can't threaten Him.

Second, God does not need to be defended. He can defend Himself. He can move people and nations. He can shut down and raise up. That's why the Bible says, for example, "'Vengeance is Mine, I will repay,' says the Lord" (Rom. 12:19; Deut. 32:35). He basically says, "I can do things you haven't thought about."

Third, God does not depend on us. He enjoys us and wants our worship and fellowship, as we will see. But when you come to know God, you have to bank on Him, not the other way around.

I don't know of any more important statement I can make than this: God's sufficiency means that we can find our completeness only in Him. This truth appears all through the Bible, but I want to take one of the most beautiful poetic passages in Scripture to make an all-important point.

David wrote Psalm 23 while reflecting on his previous occupation as a shepherd. David knew God. The Psalms reflect his intimacy with God and his knowledge of God. God Himself said that David was a man after His own heart. As he reflected, David realized that what he was as a shepherd to his sheep, God was to him.

So David wrote, "The LORD is my shepherd, I shall not want" (v. 1). He says that if you really come to understand who God is, if you begin to live in the light of who God is rather than who you think God is, if you simply let God be God, you will have no lack. Many of us are failing in our lives because we want to make God into a glorified man. David is essentially saying, "Let God be God." In making this statement, we are recognizing that only God is self-sufficient, and we are not.

When sheep try to make shepherds into sheep, the sheep are going to be confused. But as long as sheep let the shepherd be the shepherd, they will have someone to lead them where they ought to go. Sheep cannot take the place of shepherds nor can sheep become shepherds. Likewise, shepherds do not want to become like sheep. Each has a distinct role.

Stop trying to get God to be like you, and simply let God be God, as He defines Himself to be.

When you do that, He will let you be you as you ought to be. David says, "I shall not want." The remainder of the Psalm then explains that if the Lord is your shepherd, He will meet every category of need you will ever have. You may doubt that He will, but God never doubts. In fact, God never doubts Himself. He doesn't scratch His head and say, "I wonder whether I can pull this off." He never says, "Oops!"

That being so, it's no wonder He has asked us to trust Him, because He trusts Himself. He knows what His name "I AM THAT I AM" truly means, even when we are unable to comprehend the various truths on God's attributes.

This holiest of names for God, known as the *tetragrammaton*, is the name of God that He gave Himself directly in revealing it to humanity. In fact, the name is made up of four consonants and no vowels, making it impossible to pronounce. It was viewed so holy in the biblical days that the Israelites could not and would not dare speak it. So, to give it a way to be pronounced, they took some vowels to create the name Yahweh. Yahweh's root is in this name YHWH. This "I AM THAT I AM" nature of God speaks to His holiness. It speaks to His transcendence. But it also speaks to His eternality. As we read in Psalm 90:1–2, "Lord, You have been our dwelling place in all generations. Before the mountains were born or You gave birth to the earth and the world, even from everlasting to everlasting, You are God."

This profound truth we discover about God's attributes speaks to His present reality. According to the Scripture we just read that Moses penned in Psalms, "from everlasting to everlasting"—God has always existed. When did God begin? From everlasting. But if you exist from everlasting, you have no starting point.

To put it another way, there has never been a time when God was not. Now, don't try to figure that one out, or it will cause your brain to truly struggle. I remember when I was a young Christian, and I just stood in my room one day thinking about the fact that God has no beginning. But how can something not have a beginning?

The evolutionists say that out of nothing a beginning happened. They give a lot of different reasons such as the "Big Bang" or cosmic energy or primordial slime. But they try to argue that something came out of nothing. I'll stick with God because everyone has the same problem: Who or what is the first cause here?

God existed from everlasting. There never was a time when

God was not, and there will never be a time when God will not be. It is very important to realize that God is forever. This truth has a fundamental implication for us: With God, there is no such thing as the succession of events. History is a meaningless concept to Him but very important for us.

We are creatures of history because we are linear creatures. We go from point A to point B to point C. We go from this event to that event to the next event, one after the other. We are creatures of the past, the present, and the future. We are linear, successive creatures, but God is not. He knows about history because He's the God of history, but history doesn't define Him.

The eternality of God also means that God is independent. Everything created needs something outside itself to exist. But God depends on nothing outside Himself to exist. He is self-generating.

Now I've got good news and bad news.

The bad news is God does not need us. He did not create us out of any need or lack in His being. Before there was earth or anything else, God was. When the earth was created, God had already existed zillions of years. In fact, even that is an understatement, since one can go back into eternity forever and never find a time when God did not exist. How did He make it that long without us? Because God needs nothing outside Himself to be Himself or to be complete. He is totally self-generating. He is totally fulfilled within Himself.

The good news is that God created us so we could get in on what He is enjoying: Himself. He created us so we can enjoy Him, benefit from Him, and participate in His world, not to make up for something that was lacking in Himself.

GOD IS AN IMMUTABLE BEING

God is not only transcendent, eternal Spirit; He is also immutable. *Immutability* means not having the ability to change. "Every good thing given and every perfect gift is from above, coming down from the Father of lights, with whom there is no variation or shifting shadow" (James 1:17).

God cannot, does not, will not change. That makes Him unlike everything in creation. The second law of thermodynamics says that every transformation of energy is accompanied by a loss of available energy, so that future use of that energy is no longer available to the same degree. In other words, people change, clothes change, seasons change, times change, hair changes, and shoes change. But God does not change. His Word does not change. Psalm 119:89 says, "Forever, O LORD, Your word is settled in heaven."

The writer of Hebrews testifies that God's purpose is unchangeable (immutable, incapable of change), and to prove it, God swore "by two unchangeable [immutable] things in which it is impossible for God to lie" (Heb. 6:17–18). God's character does not change. Neither does His love (Jer. 31:3). The Son of God does not change, for "Jesus Christ is the same yesterday and today and forever" (Heb. 13:8). God's plans do not change (Ps. 33:11), and His knowledge is the same today as it was on the day He created the world.

Do you get the point? God does not, cannot, and will not ever change. Let's go back to James 1:17: "Father of lights" means that God is the Father of the moon, the stars, the sun, the lights in heaven. He's not one of the lights. We don't worship the moon. He is the lights' "Daddy." He made them. Then James throws in a wonderful line about God: "with whom there is no variation or shifting shadow." That's sweet.

Every day, we have to deal with shadows because the earth, rotating on its axis around the sun, shifts the light of the sun every twenty-four hours. We have a shadow on our side of the earth at dusk because of the earth's rotation. Several hours later, that shadow will turn to darkness. If it were not for the lights up in the heavens (and, in modern times, artificial light), you would be able to see virtually nothing at night.

But then the next morning, that shadow will disappear again. It will be daylight here and night somewhere else, a never-ending process. But God is not like our twenty-four-hour time period. He does not move from dark to light, from night to day. He is constant. That's why heaven has no night, no "shifting shadow," since God Himself is the light. It will not be light today and dark tomorrow because God's nature is consistent. He is immutable.

Whenever we talk about God's immutability, someone always says, "Wait a minute. The Bible talks about God changing His mind. In fact, He changed His mind about destroying Israel after Aaron built the golden calf."

That's true as far as it goes. The Bible does say that God was going to destroy the people for their sin (Ex. 32:10). But Moses pleaded with God not to do it: "So the LORD changed His mind about the harm which He said He would do to His people" (v. 14).

Let me add another one to that. God also changed His mind concerning Nineveh (Jonah 3). He said that He was going to destroy the city in forty days (v. 4), and then He changed His mind. So we've got a problem here. If God doesn't change, how can He change His mind?

Although God's character does not ever change, His methods may. Here's what I mean. God's character is constant; however, if a change on man's part affects another part of God's character, God is then free to relate to that person out of that facet of His character rather than out of the another facet of His character.

For example, God was going to destroy Nineveh because of its sin. God does not change His mind about sin. But what changed was that the people of Nineveh repented. When they did, they appealed to another part of God's character, His grace and mercy. God was dealing with them from one part of His changeless character, His wrath against sin. But their repentance brought them under another part of His changeless character.

So God "changed" only in that He allowed the Ninevites' actions to pull in another part of who He is. God doesn't change in His essence, but He changes in His methods and His actions based on our willingness to adjust. It's not God who adjusts. He reacts to our adjustment. When you get right with God, you appeal to another aspect of His character—but that character never changes because it is already perfect.

By the way, God has given us proof that He will never change: the rainbow. The rainbow was God's promise to Noah that He would never destroy the earth by water again. Destroying mankind in the flood grieved God so bad that He said, in effect, "I'll never do it again, and to let you know that, I'll give you a rainbow as a sign in the heavens." Every time you see a rainbow, you can be reminded of this changeless aspect of God and the peace this truth provides you.

Knowing and understanding the attributes of God will take you deeper in your spiritual walk than any other pursuit. It is in knowing Him that you know all other things because He is the source of all things. In fact, you will access spiritual power through knowing Him. As Daniel 11:32 says, "but the people who know their God will display strength and take action." All boasting must be rooted only in the knowing and understanding of God (1 Cor. 1:28–31). He has made this knowing available to you and me through Jesus Christ so as to nullify the things of this world order. Yet, while knowing Him is an available pursuit for each of us, we will never fully know God until we transition to heaven (1 Cor. 13:12) and even then it will take all eternity to fully come to know our inexhaustible God.

King David said it best when he penned Psalm 139:6: "Such knowledge is too wonderful for me; it is too high, I cannot attain to it." That is not to say we are to give up the quest. Rather, it is to propel us forward as David also wrote about his soul resembling that of a deer panting for the water brooks (Ps. 42:1).

I applaud your search to know God more. It is a search we are on together as we explore, study, dissect, discern, and come to experience more fully the many attributes of our great and awesome God.

Chapter 2

THE ALLNESS OF GOD

O ne of the preeminent attributes that forms our foundation
of knowing God includes the attribute of His allness. By
allness, I refer to His ability to be all in all. Larger theological
terms for this include *omniscience, omnipresence,* and *omnipotence.* While those words may feel large and foreign, what they
mean ought to resonate easily within.

The "omni" (i.e., allness) attributes of God operate in tandem with each other. For instance, God can do anything He
wants to do (He's omnipotent) anywhere He wants to do it because He's everywhere (He's omnipresent). God knows everything there is to know (He's omniscient) because all knowledge
originates from somewhere, and God is present in every one of
those places.

More than that, God can do with that knowledge whatever
He chooses because His omnipotence gives Him the power to
act on what He knows. And since He is omnipresent, He is al-

ways wherever He needs to be to do whatever needs to be done. God's full-orbed character allows Him to function in every sphere of existence.

But to understand each aspect of this attribute of allness more fully, let's look at them one by one. We can start with God's omniscience.

GOD IS OMNISCIENT

The omniscience of God means that there is absolutely nothing He doesn't know; that no informational system or set of data exists anywhere outside of God's knowledge—nothing. He depends on no one outside Himself for any knowledge about anything.

In Isaiah 40:13–14, the prophet gives us this tremendously valuable piece of information about God's perfect knowledge:

> Who has directed the Spirit of the LORD,
> Or as His counselor has informed Him?
> With whom did He consult and who gave Him
>   understanding?
> And who taught Him in the path of justice and taught
>   Him knowledge,
> And informed Him of the way of understanding?

Isaiah raises the question to illustrate a fundamental principle: God does not gain His knowledge by learning. He does not need to study, read, and analyze. He knows what He knows simply because He knows it. All knowledge on all subjects are intrinsically known to Him. He did not learn it. Everything that can be known, everything that has ever been known, and everything that will ever be known, He already knows.

The Bible says, for example, that "the very hairs of your head are all numbered" (Matt. 10:30). I realize for some people, that's an easy count. But the point is that God knows the number of hairs on your head not because He counted them, but because He is God and He knows. This knowledge exists for every person on the planet (see John 1:9).

Because God is an eternal being, whatever He knows, He knows immediately and simultaneously. Because He is eternal, He does not have to look back to the past to remember or look forward to the future to project. All knowledge—past, present, and future—resides in Him in the eternal now. All that is known, has been known, will be known, could be known, or has been forgotten, God knows intuitively and eternally.

This gets very personal. God knows that you are reading this book at this moment. He knows what you are thinking about as you read. When you sit in church, He knows whether you'd rather be somewhere else. He knows what you plan to do when you leave church. He is acutely aware of all data at all times that pertains to all people everywhere and He does not even have to "google" it.

All the information in all the libraries of the world; all the data on all the computer chips in the world, including the K-wave quantum computers and those that have not yet been made; all of this data, God knows perfectly and completely right now. Because He is infinite, "His understanding is infinite" (Ps. 147:5).

I like the way the author of Hebrews put it when he wrote, "And there is no creature hidden from His sight, but all things are open and laid bare to the eyes of Him with whom we have to do" (Heb. 4:13). Nothing can be hidden from God. He knows our feelings, our desires, our excuses, and our personalities. He knows everything and anything, and He knows it comprehensively. Nothing sits outside of the body of information He possesses. According to Acts 15:18, He has known everything from the very beginning. Needless to say, it would be quite difficult to give God a surprise party, for 1 John 3:20 also affirms that He knows all things.

God's comprehensive knowledge also includes a moral element. Proverbs 15:3 says that "the eyes of the LORD are in every place, watching the evil and the good." Nothing can escape His all-encompassing knowledge—not the biggest or the most minute detail. We saw this earlier in Matthew 10:30 in reference to the hairs of our heads.

Just one verse prior, Jesus had said, "not one [sparrow] will fall to the ground apart from your Father" (Matt. 10:29). According to Psalm 50:11, God knows every beast and every bird of the air. God's omniscience isn't confined to things on earth. The psalmist says every star among the billions of stars that inhabit all of the galaxies has been numbered and named by Him (Ps. 147:4).

God sees what's done in secret and what's done in the light. David says in Psalm 139:12 that the day and the night are alike to God. Moses reminds us that our secret sins are brought to light in His presence (Ps. 90:8). This is powerful information because it means all of our lives are totally known. He knows what's done publicly for all to see and what's done privately for none to see. This can be quite intimidating. Before Jeremiah was born, the Scripture says, God knew he would be a prophet (Jer. 1:5). In Galatians 1:15–16, Paul says he was appointed to be an apostle to the Gentiles before he was born. God knows.

God knows not only what is but also what could have been. In Matthew 11, we find Jesus pronouncing this judgment, which reveals His comprehensive knowledge, because He is God:

> "Woe to you, Chorazin! Woe to you, Bethsaida! For if the miracles had occurred in Tyre and Sidon which occurred in you, they would have repented long ago in sackcloth and ashes. Nevertheless I say to you, it will be more tolerable for Tyre and Sidon in the day of judgment than for you. And you, Capernaum. . . . will descend to Hades; for if the miracles had occurred in Sodom which occurred in you, it would have remained to this day. Nevertheless I say to you that it will be more tolerable for the land of Sodom in the day of judgment, than for you." (vv. 21–24)

Jesus says if this would have happened, then the people would have done that. That's not what happened, but Jesus said if it would have happened, this would have been the certain result. This shows how comprehensive God's omniscience is. He knows the potential as well as the actual events and outcomes of history. He alone knows the answer to every "what if" question.

The omniscience of God is not only intuitive and comprehensive but also intensely personal. It is vitally related to our day-to-day living. Psalm 139 brings this home in a very graphic way. The psalmist David begins, "O LORD, You have searched me and known me. You know when I sit down and when I rise up" (vv. 1–2).

David goes on to say, "You understand my thought from afar" (v. 2). God is acutely aware of our thinking. Ezekiel 11:5 says that God knows the thoughts that come into our mind. He knows where they came from and how they wound up there. The Bible says that God reads our hearts. He understands every thought and intent of the heart (1 Sam. 16:7).

The psalmist also says, "You scrutinize my path and my lying down, and are intimately acquainted with all my ways" (Ps. 139:3). In other words, "You scrutinize my direction in life. You look at the way I am traveling." That's why when you are lost, you can pray because God knows the right path to get you back on the right road.

"Even before there is a word on my tongue, behold, O LORD, You know it all" (v. 4). God knows your thought before it even gets into your mind. Once you have the thought, He knows how it's going to be expressed before it ever reaches your tongue. So by the time the first word gets out of your mouth, God has already waxed eloquent on that information.

No wonder David observes in verse 5, "You have enclosed me behind and before, and laid Your hand upon me." He's basically saying, "I'm locked in by Your knowledge." To put it another way, we have nowhere to run, nowhere to hide. God knows all things related to our personal lives.

One day, "Jesus saw Nathanael coming to Him, and said of him, 'Behold, an Israelite, in whom there is no deceit.'" (John 1:47). Jesus knew Nathanael's motives were pure. Even when others misread you, God knows the true story. God also knows when we act as hypocrites, wearing our masks. He knows when we look one way on the outside but are totally different on the inside. The Sadducees and Pharisees of Jesus' day went around fooling the people with their righteous talk, their righteous prayers, and their righteous fasting. But then they ran into Jesus. Being God in the flesh, He looked at them and said, "You are like whitewashed tombs . . . full of dead men's bones" (Matt. 23:27).

Jesus was referring to the Jewish law that said that anyone who touched a grave would be defiled. To avoid defilement, people would whitewash the tombs to mark them clearly so travelers could avoid them. But whitewashing a tomb didn't change the reality that it held dead people's bones. That grave was still a place of death. It was just a place of death that looked good on the outside.

God's omniscience is purposeful. The Bible says of Jesus' crucifixion that while unregenerate men killed Him, Jesus was crucified according to "the predetermined plan and foreknowledge of God" (Acts 2:23). God was ultimately responsible for the death of Jesus, even though the means He used was ungodly men. God's purpose in this was that His Son would pay for the sins of the world on the cross. Yet God's purpose also enabled humanity to have the free will to choose faith in Him for salvation.

The interplay of God's purposes with our freedom appears not only in salvation, but in our day-to-day Christian life. We find a great example in Luke 22, during the Last Supper. In the middle of the meal, Jesus turns to Peter and says, "Simon, Simon, behold, Satan has demanded permission to sift you like wheat; but I have prayed for you, that your faith may not fail;

and you, when once you have turned again, strengthen your brothers" (vv. 31–32).

Peter responds immediately, "Lord, with You I am ready to go both to prison and to death!" (v. 33). But in the very next verse, Jesus predicts Peter's failure. He basically says, "You are going to blow it. You are going to deny Me before all of these people. Satan is going to use your self-confidence to drive you to spiritual defeat. I know this in advance, so I've been praying for you."

Do you know what Jesus is doing in heaven right now? He's praying for you and me (Heb. 7:25). He's praying for us because in His omniscience He knows that at times we will go down to spiritual defeat, and He wants to deliver us from utter failure. So even though we mess up, we can get up because Jesus is praying for us. Even when He knows in advance that we will not always do what is right, He wants to keep us from doing as much wrong as we could do if He were not praying for us.

And when we do fail, God forgives us as He did Peter when we repent. God loves us in spite of our failure. If we will come back to Him, He will receive us because His love is everlasting. The only thing God chooses to forget is our sin: "I will forgive their iniquity, and their sin I will remember no more" (Jer. 31:34).

GOD IS OMNIPRESENT

There is no place in creation where God does not exist—and exist in all His divine fullness. This is the second of God's "omni" attributes we want to study concerning the "allness" of God. The word *omnipresence* itself is very simple to understand: omni means "all." Presence is a common word, having to do with locality. The omnipresence of God means that His complete essence is fully present in all places at all times.

Most people are not comfortable with an omnipresent God. That's why people like idols: they can see them, touch them, and, most important, control them. Even some people who go to church do not want to worship the God of the Bible. They come to His house of worship, but then they go back to their idols. It could be their money, cars, prestige, power, clothes, or notoriety, but they want something they can control. Some have taken this to extremes and created entire theological systems in an attempt to confine, limit, or control God.

The omnipresence of God teaches us that our God dwells intimately in history and yet exists totally outside of history. He is both transcendent and immanent at the same time. In 1 Kings 8, Solomon dedicates the magnificent temple he built as a dwelling place for the glory of God so that Israel will know it is God's house. But Solomon did not want the people to get confused and think that God's presence was limited to their building. So he prays,

> "Now therefore, O God of Israel, let Your word, I pray, be confirmed which You have spoken to Your servant, my father David.
>
> But will God indeed dwell on the earth? Behold, heaven and the highest heaven cannot contain You, how much less this house which I have built!" (vv. 26–27)

God's presence is in the sphere of immensity and infinitude. *Infinitude* or *infinity* refers to that which is without limit. *Immensity* refers to that which cannot be contained. God's presence is so vast that he not only is everywhere in the known universe but bursts through the limits of the universe and fills everything we do not even know about. When man tries to stuff God into the universe, Solomon effectively says to God, "You burst out of it. It cannot contain You."

God's presence is also distinct in that all of Him exists everywhere. He is not broken up into parts. The entire presence of God exists in each little piece of the universe. We know this because God's being is characterized by what theologians call "simplicity." That is, He cannot be divided.

God is spirit. He's an uncompounded being. So everything everywhere is encompassed by the presence of God. But He is not like any human. God encompasses everything everywhere so that whatever you do, wherever you are, He is right there and all of Him is there. You don't have to worry about the fact that I am drawing on His omniscience while someone else is as well, thus limiting access. God is present everywhere in all the fullness of His deity.

It's like the air and the water. Wherever you have air, you have every component that makes air. You do not divide air. One drop of water has the same components as an ocean. Everything that makes water what it is can be found in that one drop.

The problem is sometimes we don't feel that God is with us. We can't see Him, so we wonder whether He's there. But we experience many things we don't see, like a chilly morning or the blowing of the wind. We know the wind is blowing because we see and feel its effects all around us. We have to put on a coat to keep off the chill, or struggle to keep the wind from turning our umbrellas inside out. Because of what God has done that we do see, we can be confident of His reality when He appears to be doing nothing, just like we are confident in the reality of air even when the wind is not blowing.

This is why the Bible says, "The fool has said in his heart, 'There is no God'" (Ps. 14:1). Only a fool would say to himself, "It's not chilly," or, "It's not windy," when all the evidence points to the contrary, and all he has to do to confirm it is go outside and feel the cold. Similarly, such a person would be foolish to deny the reality of air when the wind is not blowing. God is everywhere. David raises a vital question in Psalm 139 when he asks,

> Where can I go from Your Spirit?
> Or where can I flee from Your presence? (v. 7)

Then he begins to speculate on what he would find if he went to the farthest corners of the universe:

> If I ascend to heaven, You art there;
> if I make my bed in Sheol, behold, You are there.
> If I take the wings of the dawn,
> If I dwell in the remotest part of the sea,
> Even there Your hand will lead me,
> And Your right hand will lay hold of me. (vv. 8–10)

No matter where he went, David knew that he would run into the sustaining hand and presence of God.

The good thing about God is He's so big you can't get over Him, but He's so close you can't get away from Him. That means He's near you today. I don't know what you are facing, but He's right beside you—and because He's omniscient, He knows what's going on. He's not a "do nothing" God.

God is intimately involved and ever-present in your life and therefore aware of all you are going through. As the Bible says in Acts 17:28, "in Him we live and move and exist." In the same way air surrounds us, we are surrounded by God.

Yet even though God is equally present everywhere in all of His fullness, He is not equally related to everyone and every-thing. In other words, we have an equality of *essence*, but not of *relationship*. God relates to things and people differently, even though He exists equally with them all. The Bible says, for ex-ample, that people need to call on God "while He is near" (Isa. 55:6). That statement does not refer to God's essence but to the way He relates to people.

Again, the prophet says that God's people "remove[d] their hearts far from Me" (Isa. 29:13). This is a moral and spiritual statement, since no one can get away from an omnipresent God. God the Father was present when Jesus died on the cross, yet we know that Jesus looked up and said, "My God, my God, why hast thou forsaken Me?" (Matt. 27:46 KJV)

The Bible teaches that God adjusts His presence, so to speak, to things and people based on how He is related to them. Isaiah 43:1–7 brings this out very directly:

> But now, thus says the LORD, your Creator, O Jacob,
> And He who formed you, O Israel,
> "Do not fear, for I have redeemed you;
> I have called you by name; you are Mine!
> "When you pass through the waters, I will be with you;
> And through the rivers, they will not overflow you.

When you walk through the fire, you will not be scorched,
Nor will the flame burn you.
"For I am the LORD your God,
The Holy One of Israel, your Savior;
I have given Egypt as your ransom,
Cush and Seba in your place.
"Since you are precious in My sight,
Since you are honored and I love you,
I will give other men in your place and other peoples in
   exchange for your life.
"Do not fear, for I am with you;
I will bring your offspring from the east,
And gather you from the west.
"I will say to the north, 'Give them up!'
And to the south, 'Do not hold them back.'
Bring My sons from afar,
And My daughters from the ends of the earth,
Everyone who is called by My name,
And whom I have created for My glory,
Whom I have formed, even whom I have made."

God takes care of His own. He is present with His children
in a way that He is not present with those who don't know Him.
If you know Jesus Christ, you have a special relationship with
God. He doesn't relate to you in the same way He relates to the
unredeemed sinner. God treats you as His child, as part of His
family. You enjoy the special, relational presence of God. Talk
about benefits. It's one thing to say that God is everywhere. It
is quite another to realize that because you are His child, He is
with you everywhere you go.

As a child of God, you get what nonbelievers cannot get: His special guidance. Jacob discovered that in a dramatic way in Genesis 28. He was fleeing from Esau after stealing his birthright. On his flight, he stopped for the night. With a stone for a pillow, he went to sleep and had his famous dream of the ladder going from earth to heaven and the angels of God ascending and descending on the ladder.

In his dream, Jacob also saw God standing above the ladder. God reaffirmed His covenant promises to Jacob (vv. 13–14) and then declared, "I am with you and will keep you wherever you go, and will bring you back to this land; for I will not leave you until I have done what I have promised you" (v. 15). What a promise! No wonder Jacob woke up and said, "Surely the LORD is in this place, and I did not know it" (v. 16).

God is present when you feel Him and when you don't feel Him. He is present when you sense Him and when you don't sense Him. He constantly leads you to keep His promise that He is going to do with you what He said He would do, even when it looks like He isn't doing anything with you. Even when things seem to be going wrong, they could be going just right, because when you're in God's will, the negatives are part of His positive program.

God's special, relational presence is also available to us in our needs. For example, have you ever had bills you can't pay, financial turmoil you can't handle? Hebrews 13:5 has a glorious promise for believers about His beneficial omnipresence, but an important condition is attached to it. The first half of the verse says, "Make sure that your character is free from the love of money, being content with what you have."

That's often the problem, isn't it? We are not content, and so we don't experience God's special presence. We would be further along financially today if we had been more content yesterday. But because we weren't content yesterday, we got into debt yesterday that we can't pay today. Now we don't have enough to get us through, but it's not because God didn't supply. It's because we weren't content with what He gave us.

How can we be content even though the bills keep coming? Here's the promise in the last half of verse 5: "For He Himself has said, 'I will never desert you, nor will I ever forsake you.'" It's so good, so let's keep reading to verse 6: "So that we confidently say, 'The Lord is my helper, I will not be afraid. What will man do to me?'"

You can be content with what you have because you have God's forever presence. Therefore, you don't have to be afraid of recession or inflation. You just need to be content in the apartment God has provided for you until He gives you the ability to afford a house. Paul says, "my God will supply all your needs according to His riches in glory in Christ Jesus" (Phil. 4:19). But the context of this promise discusses liberal giving to God's work.

Contentment and freedom from the love of money are what keep us from trying to turn God's promises of supply into a "health and wealth gospel." You can't command God to make you wealthy. It won't do you any good to run up a bunch of bad bills and then bring them to church in a wheelbarrow for someone to pray over them and demand that God pay them. It doesn't work like that.

I'm not saying don't try to improve or get ahead. I'm saying be content on the way there. Paul gives us invaluable insight on this in Philippians 4:11–13. He calls what he learned a "secret," and it must be a secret because so few folk seem to know about it. Whether he had nothing or was abundantly supplied, Paul had learned to be content with what God provided because he had learned, "I can do all things through Him who strengthens me" (v. 13).

He is saying that God's presence stays with you even when you are not where you want to be. More than that, God can get you where you need to go if you will do it His way. "Make sure that your character is free from the love of money." Set your spiritual priorities then look to Him and His presence.

You don't need to see God to know that He's right by your side. He only has to let the wind of His Spirit blow by you in that lonely room, or wherever you are. The good news about God's relational presence is that you can talk to Him no matter what you are doing, no matter what the time of day, no matter what your circumstance.

In your lonely time, God is present. When you are afraid, when the crime rate goes up, when you don't know how you are going to make it, or when health issues plague you or a loved one, God is with you. In Isaiah 41:10, God makes this wonderful promise: "Do not fear, for I am with you; do not anxiously look about you, for I am your God. I will strengthen you, surely I will help you, surely I will uphold you with My righteous right hand."

When life's challenges hit you, when you're facing something you've never faced before, God says, "I'm omniscient. I know what you're facing. I'm omnipresent. I'm with you as you face it. And I'm omnipotent. I can do the job. So are you going to trust yourself or trust Me? Without Me, you can do nothing."

Maybe today you don't need a new neighborhood to live in. Maybe you need to see God's angels surrounding your current neighborhood. The same thing could be said about your job, your financial circumstances, health issues, and a whole host of other things. The challenge we all face is to see God's presence surrounding us, not just to escape the trial. That's why Peter urges us to keep our conscience sensitive toward God, so that when we suffer we can know that our suffering has a purpose (1 Peter 2:19).

Let me state it once again: God is with you if you are with God. He's with you regardless in His essence, but I'm talking about His relational presence. Those of us who are married know what it means to have a mate who is there, but not there. Sometimes, a wife might look at a husband and know he's not listening to her, even though he can repeat everything she said. His mind is a million miles away. It's possible for humans to be there and yet not be there. God is present everywhere, but only His children who are committed to and following Him experience the special "there" of His comforting, strengthening, reassuring presence.

Isn't it good to know that God is there? Since that's true, we need to do what little children do when their world comes caving in. Even though they may be crying, they know whom to run to, whom to hug. God has His arms open for you.

GOD IS OMNIPOTENT

We have seen that there is nothing God does not know; that's His omniscience. There is no place He does not exist; that's His omnipresence. Additionally, there is nothing God cannot do; that's His omnipotence.

As we look at the omnipotence of God, we once again enter a realm far beyond anything we have ever experienced. All of us are concerned at one level with the issue of power. People want political power; wars are waged over power. Nature has power. Historically, we have seen the power of nature in unforgettable ways as water, wind, fire, and earthquakes have wreaked havoc on this country and around the world.

But we will see that none of these can begin to compare to the power, the omnipotence, of God. We already know that *omni* means "all." Therefore, God is all-powerful. But His omnipotence involves more than just raw power. God's omnipotence includes the exercise of His choice to use His unlimited power to reflect His divine glory and accomplish His sovereign will.

Like His other attributes, God's omnipotence has a moral base. He does not do things to impress people. He uses His power to magnify His glory and accomplish His perfect will.

God's power knows no limits. Because He is infinite, He is infinitely powerful. Since His being is unlimited, so is His power. Isaiah asks, "Do you not know? Have you not heard? The Everlasting God, the LORD, the Creator of the ends of the earth does not become weary or tired. His understanding is inscrutable" (Isa. 40:28).

The psalmists agree. David declares, "power belongs to God" (Ps. 62:11). "Great is our Lord and abundant in strength," the writer says in Psalm 147:5. That's why the Bible says that a person has to degenerate into a fool to deny that God exists and that He is extremely powerful.

All that has ever been made or that will ever be made was created by the power of God. According to Psalm 89:11, "The heavens are Yours, the earth also is Yours; the world and all it contains, You have founded them." God can create a universe because He has no limitations. He has made things we haven't even discovered yet. And when we add to this the fact that God is infinitely greater than all of His creation, we are talking about someone who is unbelievable in power.

God's power is difficult for us to grasp because of our limitations. Maybe this illustration will help. Did you know that I can lift a ton? You may not believe it, but I can. So now you're going to say, "Show me." All right, just let me hitch a ride on the next space probe that lands on the moon. Then turn on your television, and watch me lift a ton.

How can I do that? Because the law of gravity is vastly different on the moon from what it is on earth. What would be impossible for me on earth is easy on the moon because I'm in a different sphere, and I have different power. On the moon, I am limited less by the law that says, "What goes up must come down."

In other words, if you change my environment, I can do things I can't do now. We have problems with the power of God because we keep Him in our environment. We try to limit Him to what we know on earth, so we just know that He can't do this or that. But God lives in a realm far beyond us, and His power operates according to vastly different rules.

God is not only unlimited in what He can do. He is unlimited in how He gets it done. God's power is so limitless that He can create *ex nihilo*, meaning "out of nothing." He did not need raw material to put together His creation. He does not exert energy to do what He wants to get done. He doesn't strain, grunt, or groan. He doesn't get sweaty because something is too hard to lift or too difficult to make.

This is because God's power is self-generating. It can be compared to a generator that always runs and never needs fueling or fixing. God never needs anything outside Himself to generate or sustain His power. His omnipotence is such that by His speaking the word, "the heavens were made" (Ps. 33:6). "He spoke, and it was done" (v. 9), because God generates His power within Himself.

One of the best examples of God's power is the angel Gabriel's visit to Mary in Luke 1. Let me paraphrase the conversation.

The angel said, "Mary, you are going to have a baby. And what's more, He will be the Son of God!"

Mary pondered this and said, "How can this be? I'm not even married."

The angel continued, "the power of the Most High will overshadow you" (v. 35). Then he added, "And behold, even your relative Elizabeth has also conceived a son in her old age; and she who was called barren is now in her sixth month" (v. 36).

How could all of this happen? The angel had the answer: "Nothing will be impossible with God" (v. 37). The virgin birth could happen because it was God's virgin birth. If you take Him out of the picture, it's impossible. But once you include God, it's a whole new situation.

The disciples had a hard time grasping the power of God. They once watched a rich young man approach Jesus and then go away sorrowful (Mark 10:17–22). Then they heard Jesus say,

"It is easier for a camel to go through the eye of a needle than for a rich man to enter the kingdom of God" (v. 25).

That was too much, so they asked, "Then who can be saved?" (v. 26).

Jesus answered, "With people it is impossible, but not with God; for all things are possible with God" (v. 27).

People often say that God has to show them His power before they'll believe. But He has shown us His power. The evidence of it surrounds us. God asked Job a very interesting question:

"Where were you when I laid the foundation of the earth?" (Job 38:4). God was saying, "I didn't have to get advice or help from you to pull any of this off."

Think about this. It takes no more effort for God to create a universe than it does for Him to create an ant. All He has to do is say, "Ant be," and you've got an ant. He says, "Universe be," and you've got a universe. No effort is involved here.

The prophet Jeremiah says, "Ah Lord God! Behold, You have made the heavens and the earth by Your great power and by Your outstretched arm! Nothing is too difficult for You" (Jer. 32:17).

Once you know God can make the universe, you know nothing else is difficult for Him. If He can pull that off, He can do anything because the universe includes everything. God's power is broad in its scope and sweep. He has power over nature. That's why you cannot equate the power of God with nature.

If you don't believe God has power over nature, ask Pharaoh. Ask the children of Israel, who went through the Red Sea and saw God hold back nature and then collapse it on the Egyptians.

Ask the people of Sodom and Gomorrah after the brimstone fell from heaven to destroy those two cities. Ask Noah's family after it rained for forty days and forty nights. Ask the disciples who were in the boat with Jesus when He said, "Peace, be still!"

Not only does God have power over nature, but His power is so broad that it sustains as well as creates things. The author of Hebrews puts it this way: "He [Jesus] is the radiance of His [the Father's] glory and the exact representation of His nature, and upholds all things by the word of His power" (Heb. 1:3).

The word "upholds" means "to sustain." The earth doesn't spin out of its orbit because God keeps it intact. We don't burn or freeze to death because God keeps the sun at just the right distance from us. God upholds things by the word of His power. He keeps them on track. He keeps them going. He holds the universe together. He can keep your life together because He is the great Sustainer.

Let's return to Psalm 139. We keep coming back to this psalm as we talk about these "omni" attributes of God because it talks about all three: God's omniscience, His omnipresence, and His omnipotence. David is meditating on the greatness of God, and he says in verses 13–14: "For You formed my inward parts; You wove me in my mother's womb. I will give thanks to You, for I am fearfully and wonderfully made."

Any doctor will tell you that the two cells that come together in a mother's womb already carry the DNA code to determine the baby's race, height, and every other trait down to the shape of his or her nose. God has to know what He's doing to pull that off! He has to be powerful.

God's power is seen in His ability to create life. It's also seen in His ability to handle those who try to destroy life—demons. In Matthew 8:28–34, Jesus came upon two demon-possessed men. They had lost their minds and turned violent as a result of this demonic oppression. The demons saw Jesus and cried out, knowing what His power could do to them. So the demons asked Jesus for permission to leave the men and go into a herd of pigs nearby. Jesus dismissed the demons, who entered the herd of pigs and destroyed them.

The devil wants to destroy you, but someone has more power than the devil and his entire realm, and that is God. He is the only One who can dismiss those things that will drive you crazy and tear you apart.

God also has power over circumstances. This is another of the wonderful lessons that Jeremiah learned. God told the prophet, "I'm going to judge Israel by bringing the Babylonians in to destroy the nation and carry you off." But with the city of Jerusalem under siege by the Babylonians, God told Jeremiah to buy himself a plot of land (see Jer. 32:6–9).

Jeremiah obeyed and bought the land, although as he thought about it later, it seemed to make about as much sense as arranging deck chairs on the Titanic. In verse 25, he expressed his misgivings to God. After all, wasn't Israel about to be carried off into captivity? What good would a piece of land do Jeremiah?

The prophet was distressed. His circumstances were bad, but God had another word for him. First, though, the Lord needed to establish some ground rules. So He asked Jeremiah, "Behold, I am the LORD, the God of all flesh; is anything too difficult for Me?" (v. 27). This was not a multiple-choice question, so Jeremiah knew the answer had to be no.

Why did God make this declaration of His omnipotence? Because He was about to tell Jeremiah that when the captivity of Israel was finished, He would bring the nation back to its land and the people would enjoy prosperity again (vv. 36–44). Then Jeremiah's deed would mean something. The negative was not the last word because God has power over circumstances.

But God just doesn't go around showing you how strong He is. He does what He does for a reason. He has purposes tied to His power. That's why you don't get everything you want—not because He can't, but because it's not best. It is not His will. It doesn't magnify His glory. God's omnipotence is guided by His love, wisdom, and sovereign purposes.

You can never detach God's omnipotence from His sovereignty. Revelation 19:6 puts it this way: "Hallelujah! For the Lord our God, the Almighty, reigns." That is, His omnipotence is tied to His rule, and His rule is tied to His will. So to get His power, you must be tied to His will. If you are not in the will of God, you won't experience the beneficial power of God because God always exercises His power with a purpose.

Jesus understood this. According to Hebrews 5:7, Jesus cried out to His Father, knowing that the Father had the power to deliver Him from death. Jesus, in His humanity, did not want to die on that cross, but in the Garden of Gethsemane we find Him praying, "yet not what I will, but what You will" (Mark 14:36). With God, it's never a question of power. The issue is matching His power with His will. We need to ask God, "What does Your ruling power wish to do?" That should be our major concern, finding and getting in line with the will of God. God's desires are never more extensive than His powers. He says in Isaiah 46:10,

"My purpose will be established, and I will accomplish all My good pleasure." God uses His power to accomplish His will.

Here's the best part. The ones who really get to see God's power are His people. I like Ephesians 3:19–20. Paul prays that we might comprehend the love of Christ and "be filled up to all the fullness of God." Then in verse 20, Paul says, "Now to Him who is able to do far more abundantly beyond all that we ask or think, according to the power that works within us."

If you ever forget the word *omnipotent*, if the word *power* doesn't do anything for you, just do what the writers of the Bible did. They reached back to an old phrase and simply said, "He's able." If you lose all the theology of it, if you don't know how to match omnipotence with sovereignty, just remember this phrase: "He's able."

In his magnificent benediction in Ephesians 3:20, Paul is simply saying, "He's able." That's all I'm saying. God is able. Despite your circumstances, God's power is very personal to you. He's able, and if you can think it or ask it, He can do it (and more) because He's able.

Let me show you four final things you need to know about God's omnipotence:

1. *God must have your fully committed heart.* He doesn't want you to be divided. He doesn't want you committed to Him on Sunday and to the world on Monday. He doesn't want you to be two-timing Him. "The eyes of the LORD move to and fro throughout the earth that He may strongly support those whose heart is completely His" (2 Chron. 16:9). Think about it. God is trying to find someone through whom to show His power.

2. *You must also have faith.* But you might say, "My faith is weak." Well, in Mark 9, Jesus was met by a father who wanted his son healed. He made a pretty weak statement of his faith to Jesus: "If You can do anything, take pity on us and help us" (v. 22).

Jesus immediately challenged that, and the man cried out, "I do believe; help my unbelief" (v. 24). This man was saying, "I kind of believe. I want to believe. I need to believe, but my belief system is not working right today."

Jesus healed the boy anyway because the father was willing to bring his unbelief to Christ and let Him turn it into belief. So even if your faith isn't working right, if you bring your weak faith to a mighty God, that's all the faith you need because He's able. He doesn't need perfect faith from you in order to work; He merely needs you to stop trusting yourself and be willing to trust Him.

3. *The Bible also says you need to be humble* (*1 Peter 5:5–6*). We know that God has always been opposed to the proud, but He gives victory to the humble. So if you are going to experience His omnipotent power and discover for yourself that He's able, you must be humble and willing to submit to Him.

4. *You must be ready to wait on the Lord.* The prophet Isaiah says,

> Do you not know? Have you not heard?
> The Everlasting God, the LORD, the Creator of the ends of
>   the earth
> Does not become weary or tired.
> His understanding is inscrutable.
> He gives strength to the weary,
> And to him who lacks might He increases power.

Though youths grow weary and tired,

And vigorous young men stumble badly,

Yet those who wait for the LORD

Will gain new strength;

They will mount up with wings like eagles,

They will run and not get tired,

They will walk and not become weary. (Isa. 40:28–31)

Does "wait on the Lord" mean sit and do nothing? No. It means don't rely on human schemes. "Wait on the Lord" means do it God's way, not your way. It means not going outside of God's revealed will to achieve your goals and desires. Many of us have not seen God's power because we are too busy trying to create our own power. We haven't seen God's power because we are too busy concocting our own schemes.

We haven't seen God pay the bills, for example, because we believe the only one that can help us is MasterCard, American Express, or Visa. We keep using our power, so we never get around to seeing God's power. And God will not share power with anyone.

Our churches ought to be filled every week with believers ready to testify about the power of God: how He made them love someone they didn't think they could love; how He gave them the ability to meet a need they didn't think they could meet; how He turned their circumstances around. We ought to be willing to go before the Lord, even if it means fasting and praying, and say, "I can't, Lord, but You can. You're able."

We're often like the little boy whose father told him to pick up a heavy rock that was in their way. The boy tried, grunted, and said, "Daddy, I can't lift it."

His daddy said, "Yes, you can."

The boy tried again. "Ughhhh. Daddy, I can't lift it."

"Yes, you can."

The boy went back again. Same result. "Daddy, I can't lift it!"

"Yes, you can. You're not using all your strength."

This went on two or three more times, the boy insisting that he was using all his strength. Finally, the father put his arm around the boy and said, "Son, you don't understand. You did not use all your strength. You did not ask me."

God can pick up the rocks in your life, but you've got to ask Him. He can move the heavy rocks in your marriage, your job, your health, or your family, but you've got to ask Him. He doesn't want you grunting and groaning in your own strength because He already knows, "Without Me, you can do nothing."

God is able. In His allness, He can do all.

Chapter 3

THE HOLINESS OF GOD

A woman in an ice-cream shop places her order. As she waits to receive it, she turns around and spots a famous actor. She has admired this actor for many years, so his presence obviously captures her attention. Seeing him causes her to become instantly speechless. Taking her change and her ice cream, she shuffles by him on her way out the door with a look of amazement on her face.

Once she gets out the door, though, she notices that she didn't have her ice cream after all. Both hands are empty. She muses that the wonder of seeing this actor had caused her to forget why she had been in there. But as she was musing, the actor walks out of the parlor with his own ice cream in hand. "You don't have your ice cream, do you?" he asks her with a smile on his face.

"No," she replies, "I forgot it," surprised she is able to form words at all.

"Oh, you didn't forget it," he calmly assures her. "You stuck it in your purse with your change."

The lady instantly looks down to see her melting ice cream cone right there in her purse! She had become so overwhelmed by the presence of greatness that she had lost continuity with her own ability to make sense of her actions.

The Bible tells about a similar experience of someone becoming overwhelmed by greatness. When the prophet Isaiah encountered this next attribute of God—which we are going to look at in this chapter—he could barely stand. God's holiness "undid" Isaiah, in his own words (Isa. 6:5 KJV). To "undo" someone simply means to unravel them at their very core. God's holiness is more than we, as humans, can even grasp.

No other attribute of God revealed to us throughout Scripture is emphasized like this one. There exists no alternate characteristic that is expressed to the third degree like this one. God is never called "Love, Love, Love." Nor is He called "Peace, Peace, Peace." He's not even called "Truth, Truth, Truth."

But He is called "Holy, Holy, Holy," as He was called in the presence of Isaiah. This attribute of His holiness is the only one spoken of to that degree, and receives this level of emphasis because it runs through all the others. Its uniqueness shows up in the reality that all the other attributes are defined by this one. For example, God's love is holy. His truth is holy. His Word is holy. His ways are holy. His law is holy. His name is holy. His nature is holy. I could go on and on, but I think you get the point. Throughout the Bible, you will find the attribute of holiness established with all the other attributes.

What makes this attribute unique as the nucleus of God,

then, is that everything about Him is this attribute.

God is holy. From Genesis to Revelation, God is described as holy. The concept is inescapable. His holiness cannot be missed. In fact, God's holiness reigns so supremely dominant that He has a whole book on it—the book of Leviticus. Leviticus distinguishes between the profane, the common, and the holy. The profane is that which is dirty and sinful. The common is that which is regular and ordinary. The holy, however, is the "no-trespassing" sign God puts around His uniqueness. It is like having dirty dishes in the sink (the profane), regular dishes in the kitchen cupboard (the common), but the special china in its own glass case in its own dining room cabinet. It is not for regular use. It is set apart as unique. God's holiness means He is unique and separate from that which is inconsistent with His nature. He must be treated as special and in a class by Himself.

God's holiness (His uniqueness, separateness, and distinctiveness) is a beautiful thing, which is why we are called to worship Him in the beauty of holiness (1 Chron. 16:29; 2 Chron. 20:21; Ps. 29:2; 96:9). Just as the sun exposes the beauty of creation, God's holiness demonstrates how awesome He is in all the perfections of His being.

Exodus 15 shows a great picture of God's holiness as Moses and the sons of Israel sing about their deliverance from Pharaoh and his army. In verses 8–10, the singers begin reciting what we might call *poetic-anthropomorphisms* (human features used to describe God). We read of His power in simply blowing through His nostrils and piling up the waters on both sides. Having recited Israel's great deliverance, Moses then says, "Who is like You among the gods, O Lord? Who is like You, majestic in holiness, awesome in praises, working wonders?" (v. 11). Essentially, Moses explains that if you want to understand the majesty, distinctiveness, and uniqueness of God, you have to understand it in concert and cadence with His holiness.

The prophet Isaiah writes,

> For thus says the high and exalted One who lives forever, whose name is Holy, "I dwell on a high and holy place, and also with the contrite and lowly of spirit in order to revive the spirit of the lowly and to revive the heart of the contrite." (57:15)

God says He dwells on high in a holy place because He is the Holy One. The Hebrew word "holy" means "separate." It is the same root word from which we get the words "saint" or "sanctified." All of these carry the meaning "to be separate or distinct." Because God is distinct from His creation, we must humble ourselves before Him. And because He is so high in where He dwells, He has to bow low in order to convene with each of us. It is this reality that fosters our own humility.

That is why God told Moses at the burning bush, "Remove your sandals from your feet, for the place on which you are standing is holy ground" (Ex. 3:5). When you come to understand how high and holy God is, you will come to understand how little we are. A dismissive attitude about God reveals not only a misconception of yourself, but also a terrible misconception of God.

The Bible makes clear in Romans 10:3 that people are ignorant of the holiness of God. And 1 John 1:5 teaches that they do not understand that "God is Light, and in Him there is no darkness at all." He is perfect in holiness. James 1:13–14 says that God cannot sin. He cannot even be tempted to sin, and He cannot tempt someone else to sin. The very idea of sin either in God or coming from God is inconceivable because of His purity.

We must understand this because we tend to get really confused here. We grade sin by degrees. We say, "He's a bad sinner, a murderer, a rapist." Then we climb the ladder a little bit and say, "Well, he's an 'okay' sinner. He's not all that hot, but he's not like that bad sinner." Then we climb up a little higher and come to the 'good' sinner, "He's a nice guy. He's not perfect, but he's cool." Finally, we come to the 'excellent' sinner. That's where most of us think we stand. We say, "Yeah, I'm not perfect, but Lord have mercy, I'm good!"

We make these measurements, but God recognizes no such measurement. He has no degrees of sin.

Now don't misunderstand me. There are many degrees of consequences. Every sin doesn't deserve the same penalty, but evil does not have degrees. The man on death row is no different in the sight of a holy God from the person who goes through all of his life and tells only one lie. This is fundamental. God does not have a grading system for sin because He is totally and absolutely perfect in all His ways. He knows no gradations of sin.

Suppose you were sick, and as the doctor was getting ready to operate on you, he said, "All my scalpels are dirty. I've got one that I just picked up out of the mud. It's real dirty. I've got another one here that I cleaned, but I smeared some of the dirt on it. It's a little better, but it's still dirty. But I've got this one scalpel that's just got a little spot of dirt on it. So I think we can chance this operation on you with this scalpel that has only a little spot."

But that little spot can be as bad as the thick dirt. Why? Because it takes only a few germs to contaminate your whole body. You want to make sure the doctor's scalpel has been sterilized. You want absolute cleanliness when it comes to cutting you open. God is so holy—His scalpel so absolutely clean—that He is as offended by an evil thought as He is by murder. While there are differences in the consequences of sin, there is no difference in essence.

That's how holy, how totally unlike us, God is. We have to do the adjusting. He's not going to change.

When you come to understand the holiness of God, something has to happen. When the prophet Habakkuk ran into the holiness of God, he said, "My inward parts trembled . . . my lips quivered. Decay enters my bones" (Hab. 3:16). He had a different view of himself.

When Job encountered the holiness of God, he cried out, "Behold, I am insignificant. . . . I lay my hand on my mouth" (Job 40:4). Later he said, "I repent in dust and ashes" (42:6). And Job was a good man. God said so (see Job 2:3).

When Isaiah beheld God's holiness, he could only say, "Woe is me!" (Isa. 6:5). The context of when Isaiah saw God also helps in our interpretation of the passage written about the encounter. In Isaiah 6:1, we discover that Isaiah saw God in the year that the King Uzziah died. King Uzziah was the king of Israel at that time. He reigned as a great king, doing a lot of great things. Yet, unfortunately, as he began doing so many great things, he fell into the trap that many people do in the aftermath of success. King Uzziah started believing the headlines and smelling himself. Because he was the big king, admired and loved by so many, he became proud. In his pride, he made a foolish and costly mistake. We read about it in 2 Chronicles 26:16–21. Let's look at a few verses here:

> But when he became strong, his heart was so proud that he acted corruptly, and he was unfaithful to the LORD his God, for he entered the temple of the LORD to burn incense on the altar of incense. Then Azariah the priest entered after him and with him eighty priests of the LORD, valiant men. They opposed Uzziah the king and said to him, "It is not for you, Uzziah, to burn incense to the LORD, but for the priests, the sons of Aaron who are consecrated to burn incense. Get out of the sanctuary, for you have been unfaithful and will have no honor from the LORD God." But Uzziah, with a censer in his hand for burning incense, was enraged; and while he was enraged with the priests, the leprosy broke out on his forehead before the priests in the house of the LORD, beside the altar of incense (vv. 16–19).

King Uzziah had gone into the temple to burn incense before the Lord, but the spiritual rules set in place by God did not allow for that. Only priests could go inside the temple to burn incense to the Lord. Yet, because the king read his own resume one too many times, he thought he was above the rules. After all, he called the shots for most areas of the kingdom—why couldn't he call the shots for the temple as well?

Yet when the king entered the temple, he was warned to leave. Yet as quickly as his rage erupted in response, his skin ruptured with the deadly disease of leprosy. God will not stand by while His holiness is mocked through the pride of a fool, king or no king. King Uzziah would later die from this affliction.

Thus, "In the year of King Uzziah's death" (Isa. 6:1), Isaiah saw the Lord. In fact, Isaiah, "saw the Lord sitting on a throne, lofty and exalted, with the train of His robe filling the temple." Don't lose the irony here that Israel's throne room sat empty at the same time that Isaiah saw God sitting on His throne. That means, similarly, whatever is on the throne of your life that is getting in the way of God, God knows how to remove it. Whatever is being treated like God, God knows how to reduce it. And when He does, you will find out (as Isaiah did) who is really sitting on the throne after all. See, God must get rid of anything and everything that tries to take His place in your heart. King Uzziah acted out of arrogance. As a result, God dethroned him.

Before we get any deeper into this content, I want to ask you to take a moment to personally reflect. Is there a Uzziah in your life? Is there something (or someone) sitting on the throne of your thoughts and heart? Because if it infringes on God's holiness, He may remove it. Sometimes God even has to kill dreams and desires when we raise them in opposition to Him. Sometimes He has to change situations, cancel careers, or reverse finances when they seek to usurp His throne. God won't be shy to do that because His holiness demands that He be first place in each of our hearts.

The year King Uzziah died is when Isaiah got to see the Lord for who He truly is. Often, we cannot get an accurate view of God because our focus is far too fixed on what we can see. But when we do get to see Him, we will stand in awe as Isaiah did.

Here was a great prophet, but all he could say was "Woe is

me!" Isaiah was announcing a curse on himself. He was saying, "Cursed am I." Then he said, "I am ruined," or undone (v. 5). The word "ruined" means "to unravel." Isaiah basically said, "I'm coming apart," because he saw God in all His awesome holiness.

When you come face to face with God, He affects your self-esteem. You discover you are not what you thought you were when you see God. Until you see God in His holiness, you cannot see who you truly are.

If you have seen the movie *Avengers: Infinity War*, then you know what it looks like visually to "come undone." At the end of the film, superheroes and everyday people float away into utter nothingness. When Isaiah spoke woe upon himself and said he was "ruined," he was describing this unraveling. He described the ultimate emptiness within him. He was blown away.

Isaiah was also confronted with his own sin. Anytime you come face to face with God and His holiness, your own sin will be magnified in your own eyes. And even though Isaiah would be considered by most people an upstanding prophet—he didn't have a host of unruly and foolish decisions before the public—yet when standing before God, he could say nothing more than, "I am a man of unclean lips, and I live among a people of unclean lips; for my eyes have seen the King, the LORD of hosts" (Isa. 6:5).

Here we see the leading prophet condemning his own mouth. What others must have thought was his strength became the very first personal sin Isaiah points out before God. Often, it is our strengths that breed sin the most, which is why the lesson of King Uzziah is so critical for our culture today. No one—no matter how many likes, followers, or public affirmations they receive—is above God's rule in their own life. No one. King Uzziah found that out the hard way. Isaiah, when faced with God's holiness, also recognized the uncleanness in his own life.

God's holiness has a way of letting us see ourselves for who we truly are. Yet when that happens, we are to follow Isaiah's lead. Admit it. Don't try to cover it. Don't try to explain it. Don't make excuses for it. Rather, admit it. Own up to it. God knows the truth about you, so there is no point trying to talk your way out of it. You can take comfort knowing that when you confess your sins, God is faithful and just to forgive you of your sins and to cleanse you as well (1 John 1:9). Not only that, God will provide a purpose past the pain of that cleansing, as He did with Isaiah.

When Isaiah came clean with his own uncleanness, God cleaned him. We read this in verses 6–7:

> Then one of the seraphim flew to me with a burning coal in his hand, which he had taken from the altar with tongs. He touched my mouth with it and said, "Behold, this has touched your lips; and your iniquity is taken away and your sin is forgiven."

God used the heat of a burning coal to cleanse His prophet's lips. Now, keep in mind, that had to have hurt. After all, the lips are some of the softest and most sensitive parts on the entire human body. Have you ever burnt your lips with coffee or tea that was too hot? It hurts! Yet sometimes God hurts you in order to heal you. He exposes you in order to fix you. He is not doing it to be mean. He is doing it to get you to prioritize His holiness. God wants you to run after holiness like a dog chasing a rabbit—

without hesitation, fear, or distraction. That is why Hebrews 12:10 tells us that even God's discipline is meant as a way of training us in His holiness, "For they disciplined us for a short time as seemed best to them, but He disciplines us for our good, so that we may share His holiness."

And in 1 Peter 1:15–16, He says, "but like the Holy One who called you, be holy yourselves also in all your behavior; because it is written, 'You shall be holy, for I am holy.'" Our own holiness should be our highest priority. Yet often we don't realize this until we are forced into a situation like Isaiah where King Uzziah died and Isaiah stood before the Lord.

God essentially says, "Because of who I am, that is who you should strive to be." The holiness of God demands that holiness be the goal of the believer. Paul says, "Let everyone who names the name of the Lord abstain from wickedness" (2 Tim. 2:19).

If you know Jesus Christ and have been saved, your actions should be pleasing to Him. You won't always pull it off. You will fall on your face at times because you are saved sinners. But when you fall, God will forgive you if you confess your sins (1 John 1:9).

When you fall, get up in the name of Jesus Christ. His blood not only saves you, but also keeps you in contact with God. The Bible says that anyone who says he has no sin is a liar (1 John 1:8). When you come into the holy presence of God, you see more of your sin, not less of it.

If you feel like you are a worse sinner now than you were last year, it may be because you see more of God this year than you saw last year. You have seen His holiness, so now things you didn't think were wrong you recognize as wrong because they're measured against His holy standard. God wants us to build on our salvation by pursuing holiness.

You don't build a chicken coop on the foundation of a skyscraper. However, many Christians build junky lives on the foundation of the cross. Remember the Susan B. Anthony dollar? It was designed to give women a presence in the currency system, but people wouldn't use it because it looked too much like a quarter, and they kept getting the two coins mixed up.

Many of us Christians are worth a dollar, but we look like a quarter. We have a high spiritual value, but we live like "chump change." We build chicken coops on the foundation of the cross. You can't excuse sin. You can't say, "Oh, everyone does it." No, you don't know who God is.

You can't say, "Well, it was just a mistake." No, you don't know who God is.

You don't just pass it by or ignore your sin. You fall down like Isaiah and say, "Woe is me! I am undone! I am of unclean lips. Woe is me!" When Isaiah did that, the angel took the coal from the altar and put it on his lips. God cleaned Isaiah up.

Have you ever been real dirty and stepped into a nice, hot shower? You are filthy, but you get in that shower, turn on the hot water, and say with relief, "Ahhhhh!"

God tells you that you are dirty. If you will just admit you are dirty and stop thinking you are clean, He will come alongside you and scrub you so you can walk away clean, saying, "Ahhhhh!"

After God has cleaned you, He will fix you so He can use you. That is what happened to Isaiah, and that is what God will do with you if you allow Him to clean you.

We often do not take living the Christian life seriously enough because we don't know who God is. This can be compared to kids who sometimes forget who is the parent and who is the child. When they forget that, they will try anything. So every now and then, parents need to remind their children who's who. We are like children at times. We forget who God is, so we try anything.

If we are going to be serious about walking with God, we have to understand who He is and who we are in light of Him. We must go low because He sits high. We must hallow His name. We must worship Him seriously. We must stop playing church and stop playing Christianity. Most people hurry to get to work on time because they don't want to upset the boss. But they come to church saying, "As long as I get there before the benediction, I'm on time."

When God sees us treating our bosses better than we treat Him, He says, "You don't know who I am. I am the Holy One."

I will never forget the first time I went to the Grand Canyon. As far as I was concerned, it was just a big hole in the ground. Granted, it was at night when we arrived, so I couldn't see too much. But I still questioned why we had driven all that way to see what we did. That is until I saw it the next day. The daylight revealed the magnificence of the Grand Canyon. Unfortunately, far too many Christians live in the darkness of sin and miss out on getting a clear picture of not only God's holiness, but also their own lack. As a result, they live without experiencing the power of God's cleansing or the passion of His calling. After God cleansed Isaiah, He also called him to perform a great work in His name (Isa. 6:8–13). But it wasn't until Isaiah came to recognize God's holiness that he was commissioned to be sent in God's name. God wants His holiness to produce a response both within us and through us.

It wasn't until Isaiah dealt with the holiness issue in himself that he heard God's voice reveal His will for his life. As Hebrews 12:14 says, "Make every effort to live in peace with everyone and to be holy; without holiness no one will see the Lord" (NIV). Cultivating personal holiness is part and parcel to experiencing God both by hearing Him and seeing Him work in your life. God does not abide in the midst of sin.

Do you want to see God work in your life? Do you want to experience answered prayer? Do you want God to deliver you or meet a need? Then pursue His holiness. Pursue a life marked by His attribute of holiness: a life of peace, grace, kindness, contentment, purity, and forgiveness. God's desire for you is that you learn how to live as He is—holy.

So our prayer must be like that of David: "Create in me a clean heart, O God" (Ps. 51:10). In other words, "Lord, give me a clean heart. I'm dirty. I'm sinful. I've messed up, but if You will scrub me, I will be clean." This isn't a subject we often enjoy reading about or hearing a preacher speak on, but the Bible is replete with the essential nature of this attribute. God's holiness demands that we adjust, not Him. It affects everything we do, and can do.

To better understand the consequences of living in a world governed by God's holiness, let us look at God's holiness in relationship to humanity's sin.

GOD'S HOLINESS DEMANDS JUDGMENT

The holiness of God demands that He judge sin. This is repeated all through the Bible. God has always judged sin, and He has a future judgment in store, which is the Great Tribulation:

> Then I heard a loud voice from the temple, saying to the seven angels, "Go and pour out on the earth the seven bowls of the wrath of God."
>
> So the first angel went and poured out his bowl on the earth; and it became a loathsome and malignant sore on the people who had the mark of the beast and who worshiped his image.
>
> The second angel poured out his bowl into the sea, and it became blood like that of a dead man; and every living thing in the sea died.
>
> Then the third angel poured out his bowl into the rivers and the springs of waters; and they became blood. And I heard the angel of the waters saying, "Righteous are You, who are and who were, O Holy One, because You judged these things." (Rev. 16:1–5)

God judges man and creation because a holy God cannot skip over sin. He couldn't skip over it if He wanted to because He is of His holy nature. God's holiness means sin must be taken seriously and always will be judged. Even health and holiness go together. The Bible says some Christians who live a rebellious life get sick (1 Cor. 11:30; James 5:13–16). Not only that, unholiness and decay go together. Where there is unholiness, there is decay.

When we talk about the wrath or judgment of God, we do not mean mere emotional outbursts. We get mad because someone ticked us off. We get mad because we are having a bad day. God doesn't have bad days, and He doesn't just blow up. God's wrath is His natural and necessary reaction to anything and everything that is opposed to His holiness. It is natural to Him, and it is necessary because of who He is. So we are not talking about outbursts of rage. If God had outbursts, we would all be dead.

God's judgment against sin is also comprehensive. The Bible declares that God has judged and will judge Satan, and He will judge men. In fact, the Bible puts men and Satan together under judgment in Matthew 25:41. There, Jesus says: "Then [God] will also say to those on His left, 'Depart from Me, accursed ones, into the eternal fire which has been prepared for the devil and his angels.'"

God did not create hell for people. He created hell for the devil. Then why do people go there? Because they choose to follow the devil. If you choose to reject God and His salvation, you get the curse and the wrath that has been assigned to Satan. And by the way, Satan is not the "ruler" of hell, as most people think. He will be the lowest being in hell, the most severely punished. If you follow him, you follow a total loser!

God is so holy that He even judged His Son. Men crucified Jesus "by the predetermined plan and foreknowledge of God" (Acts 2:23). God's holiness is terrible. It's terrible in the Old Testament. It's terrible in the New Testament. The Bible says, "Our God is a consuming fire" (Heb. 12:29). Not was, as in the Old

Testament, but is. Our God is right now "a consuming fire." He cannot be trifled with.

We are dealing with a very holy Being who demands to be taken seriously and who stands distinct from anything that is impure. Think about it. For one sin, Adam was put out of the Garden. For one sin, Cain and his progeny were cursed. For one sin, Moses was kept out of the Promised Land. For one sin, Elijah's servant got leprosy. For one sin, Ananias and Sapphira were killed. That is "a consuming fire."

God must always have, by nature, a judgment for sin. A lot of people think, for example, that David got away with his sin. They say, "David sinned grievously, and God was gracious." That's true. David did sin, and God was gracious because David should have been executed. But did God skip over David's sin? No, He just took the lives of four of David's children in his place.

In other words, David lived because someone else died. After David sinned with Bathsheba, the baby died. I know that's hard to swallow because it is so unlike what we think God ought to be like. But that is making God in our image. God is holy by nature. The tension comes when we wrestle with the reality that God judges sin while simultaneously loving the sinner. We have to keep that tension in perspective here.

God does not wipe us all out because while He despises and judges sin, He is intensely in love with the sinner. God wants to destroy the sin without destroying the sinner. Anyone who has ever had cancer understands this. You want to nail that cancer, but you want to be able to walk away. You want to put the radiation on the cancer and wipe it out, but you want to be set free.

So God's holiness is directed against sin, but He loves the

sinner. The problem is, He cannot overlook the sinner in judging the sin because the sinner is the one doing it. The seriousness of this business of God and His holiness should shake us down to our socks. The Bible says that when God came down to the children of Israel, Mount Sinai shook. He had not even said anything yet. Just His holy presence made the mountain shake violently (Ex. 19:16–18).

Then the LORD spoke to Moses, "Go down, warn the people, so that they do not break through to the LORD to gaze, and many of them perish" (v. 21). God basically said, "If these people hang around the foot of this mountain, they are going to be in trouble. If they even try to take a peek at Me, they shall surely die."

That is our holy God.

When God moves, mountains shake. How come we are not shaking? If mountains shake when God moves, why don't we quiver, in holy reverence, at the thought of God? Why are we not reverential toward God? Why don't we hold Him in awe? Because we have forgotten who He is. We must take God seriously!

The holiness of God also means that we can approach Him on His terms alone. That is what the book of Hebrews is all about. Hebrews takes great pains to contrast the old covenant with the new covenant. And the old way of approaching God and the new way of approaching God are contrasted perhaps most graphically in Hebrews 9. Verses 21–22 sum it up:

> And in the same way he sprinkled both the tabernacle and all the vessels of the ministry with the blood. And according to the Law, one may almost say, all things are cleansed with blood, and without shedding of blood there is no forgiveness.

The fundamental principle is this: only "the shedding of blood" can satisfy the demands of a holy God. I cannot explain why that is so. I do not have all that information. I know there must be restitution. I know God requires a sacrifice. But why He chose this arrangement, I cannot fully say. All I know is that this is what God says. The very first thing that happened when Adam and Eve sinned was that God killed an animal to provide them a covering, physically and spiritually.

God is jealous for His holiness. We saw this earlier in Exodus 20:5. That is why He said, "Don't make a likeness of Me because I'm unlike anything you have ever thought of. Don't even think about it. I am a jealous God. I don't want you painting Me any less than who I really am, so just take Me at My word."

In the Old Testament, God established a comprehensive and somewhat complicated system of worship because people could not just barge into His presence. Some years ago, when George Bush was president, I was invited to the White House along with others for a briefing from the president. Can you picture me going into the White House and saying, "Is Mr. Prez in? I need to see him now."

They would say, "I'm sorry, sir, you can't see him."

"No, you don't know who I am. Tony Evans of Dallas, Texas. Pastor of Oak Cliff Bible Fellowship. We've got a radio program. I'm sure you've heard it."

They would say, "No, you don't understand. No matter who you are, he's the president."

Because of who the president is and what he represents, you don't just barge into his office. You come by invitation and permission only. It is the same with God. You don't barge into His presence. You come only because He has allowed you entrance.

God established a place and a process of worship for Israel called the tabernacle. The tabernacle was designed to let Israel know who God was—that He was distinct from them, yet He wanted to be present with them. He was different from His people, yet He wanted to be in touch with them.

The tabernacle had three different compartments, divided by three curtains. One curtain hung across the outside entrance into the court. Another curtain covered the entrance into the holy place where the sacrifices were made. The third blocked entrance into the "holiest of all" where God's presence was. Only the high priest was allowed to go in there, and only once a year.

But even the high priest couldn't just skip past the outer portions of the tabernacle to enter God's presence. Imagine him saying, "Look, I want to see God, and I want to see Him now." So he pushes past the first curtain, walks by the altar at the second curtain, and pulls back the curtain to the holiest of all. The second he crossed that threshold, he would be utterly obliterated. He would be remembered no more. And do you know why? Because he skipped the altar.

That is how serious God's holiness is. You see, unless blood was on that altar covering your sin, you better not try to go past that curtain because sinful men cannot waltz into the presence of a holy God. He doesn't allow it.

You say, "But wait a minute. How come we don't have a tabernacle?" We do! Listen to the writer of Hebrews:

> For Christ did not enter a holy place made with hands, a mere copy of the true one, but into heaven itself, now to

appear in the presence of God for us; nor was it that He would offer Himself often, as the high priest enters the holy place year by year with blood that is not his own. (9:24–25)

He goes on to say in verse 28: "So Christ also, having been offered once to bear the sins of many, will appear a second time for salvation without reference to sin, to those who eagerly await Him." Do you know why you can waltz into God's presence today? Because Jesus put His shed blood on that altar for you. You couldn't approach God any way you wanted in the Old Testament, and you can't approach Him any way you want in the New Testament.

The only reason you can approach God today is that Jesus Christ split the curtain separating us from the holiest of all. Christ opened the way so that now we have access to God through Christ (Eph. 2:18). When God sees you coming before Him, He lets you come into His presence only because He sees you through the lens of Jesus. God's condition for approaching Him is a blood sacrifice, and Jesus made that sacrifice for us.

Christ is your mediator (your go-between), your tabernacle, your only way to get into the presence of God's holiness. In Christ, each of us is granted access to stand as Isaiah did, before the Lord who is seated on His throne. We are also granted the ability, in Christ, to humbly bow and receive the cleansing forgiveness our sins require. When we do, we will be positioned to live lives of holiness in such a way, as kingdom followers, as to bring God glory and others good.

Chapter 4

THE WRATH OF GOD

What would you say about a father who failed to warn his children of impending danger? You would have to conclude that he was not being a good parent.

What would you say about a friend who saw you going down a dangerous road and knew disaster awaited you at the other end yet offered you no counsel and made no attempt to stop you? That person would be a useless friend.

How about a doctor who knew you had a life-threatening illness but simply told you, "Take two aspirin, go home, and rest"? His compassion for you as your doctor would be in serious question.

Or suppose a police officer saw smoke rising from your roof or witnessed burglars breaking into your home but never tried to intervene or alert anyone? He could be fired for failing to do his job.

Let me ask you just one more question. What would you say

about a pastor who told you about God's love and forgiveness and patience but never warned you of His wrath? That pastor would be doing you a great disservice.

God's wrath is not an easy subject to talk about. But it is as integral to His nature as His other perfections, such as His love, holiness, or mercy. If I failed to teach and write about it, I would be doing my church, my readers, and others exposed to my ministry a great disservice.

You can go plenty of places today if you don't want to hear about the wrath of God. Many churches run from the subject. They bypass it because it is difficult to talk about.

Any discussion of God's character that does not include wrath is an incomplete study. It may even be an errant study of God, because one of the very real and inescapable truths about our great God is that He is a God of wrath.

The issue is not whether we like it, want it, or agree with it. The Bible has more to say about God's wrath than it does about His love. Of course, God is good, kind, loving, and forgiving. But if you put a period there, you haven't got the complete story. God's wrath must be taken seriously. Let us begin by defining our subject: *the wrath of God is His necessary, just, and righteous retribution against sin.*

GOD IS JUDGE

God's wrath against sin arises, by necessity, out of His nature. Because of the justice of His law and the holiness of His character, God must judge sin. He takes no pleasure in punishing the unrighteous (Ezek. 33:11), but He will, because He is a God of wrath.

Psalm 18:8 puts it this way: "Smoke went up out of [God's] nostrils" as He huffed with anger at the presence of sin. Moses writes in Exodus 34:7 that God will not let the guilty go unpunished. In Deuteronomy 32:41, Moses records God's declaration that "I will render vengeance on My adversaries." Peter reminds us that God is impartial and will judge all men according to their deeds (1 Peter 1:17).

We can find no way around it, nowhere to run from it. God is a God of wrath. I want to give you the truth because it is better to have a headache now than a "hell ache" later. The Greek words for wrath indicate God's intense displeasure at sin and His judgment against it. God does not throw temper tantrums, but He has intense anger against sin.

God takes torrid displeasure at sin: big sin, little sin, medium-sized sin. He does not make a distinction between white and black lies, or between felonies and misdemeanors. Because He is a holy God, all sin is repulsive to Him. Romans 11:22 helps us here:

> Behold then the kindness and severity of God; to those who fell, severity, but to you, God's kindness, if you continue in His kindness; otherwise you also will be cut off.

The word "severity" derives from the Greek word that means "to be cut off." Paul points us to both God's goodness (the part we like to talk about) and His "cutting off" or severity.

This is a description of His wrath: when His patience against sin expires, God cuts people off from His kindness. He no longer makes His love, patience, and support available to them.

God's kindness is perfectly balanced with His severity. Both are facets of who He is.

The prophet Nahum describes God this way in the opening chapter of his prophecy:

> A jealous and avenging God is the LORD;
> The LORD is avenging and wrathful.
> The LORD takes vengeance on His adversaries,
> And He reserves wrath for His enemies.
> The LORD is slow to anger and great in power,
> And the LORD will by no means leave the guilty unpunished.
> In whirlwind and storm is His way,
> And clouds are the dust beneath His feet.
> He rebukes the sea and makes it dry;
> He dries up all the rivers.
> Bashan and Carmel wither;
> The blossoms of Lebanon wither.
> Mountains quake because of Him,
> And the hills dissolve;
> Indeed the earth is upheaved by His presence,
> The world and all the inhabitants in it.
> Who can stand before His indignation?
> Who can endure the burning of His anger?
> His wrath is poured out like fire,
> And the rocks are broken up by Him. (1:2–6)

Even after painting a picture like this, Nahum begins verse 7 by saying, "The LORD is good." God is good. But don't mistake His goodness for weakness or indifference toward sin. God is so good He cannot let evil go unaddressed.

How could God be good if He looked the other way when faced with evil? How can a police officer be good if he sees a crime and does nothing? How can a firefighter be good if he sees a fire and doesn't try to put it out? How can citizens be good if they see harm being done and do nothing?

We understand goodness to be not only positive acts, but also resistance to wrong. God's goodness contains not only the positive things He does but His negative reaction to evil. God is so good that He is going to separate sinners from saints forever. You may ask, "How is that good?"

Because if sinners in hell could visit saints in heaven, their mere presence would contaminate heaven. Instead of being a perfect place, therefore, heaven would become a living hell for the saints. God is so good that in heaven, He will keep His children separated from sin forever. We will never have to worry about being contaminated again.

In order to do this, God's wrath must be manifested. Now God's wrath is not like ours. Probably one reason people run from the subject of God's anger or wrath is that they think God gets mad the way people get mad. We get angry when someone does us wrong or when we think someone has done us wrong. We get upset when people get on our nerves, when they do something we don't like. And, too often, we respond poorly.

Yet God does not respond like that. For example, people get upset if you take something that belongs to them. Well, you can't take anything that belongs to God because He can take it back. He is all-powerful. And He knows everything in advance, so you can't trick Him. God's other characteristics keep His wrath in perfect balance.

GOD IS JUST

God's wrath is His response to that which, in its essence, is against His nature. God's wrath is not cruel, but just. Prison isn't a fun place, but we lock up people who have committed crimes to keep them from committing those crimes again because we want justice and order in society. That is a reflection—although a limited and imperfect one—of God's righteous anger.

God wants justice and order in His universe, which means He must respond to sin. God must respond to sin, and He responds by cutting the sinner off from His goodness. The Bible says these two sides of God must always be held in tension, "You have loved righteousness and hated wickedness" (Ps. 45:7).

People who talk only about the wrath of God don't have the whole picture. People who talk only about His love don't have the whole picture either. Those who want to emphasize God's love often ask this challenge to those who believe in His wrath: "How could a God of love do that?"

Simple answer: He is also a God of wrath. You cannot skip this side to God except at your eternal peril. The wrath of God is the ongoing display of His justice in history. Romans 1:18 contains the most concise statement about God's wrath in the Bible, and we do well to pay close attention to it: "For the wrath of God is revealed from heaven against all ungodliness."

Notice that God does not hide His wrath. He does not put it under a bushel. His wrath is revealed so that we can know this is part of His nature. Some people act as though God is apologetic about His anger toward sin and doesn't want us to know about it. No, the Bible says God actively reveals His wrath. He tells us in advance that this is part of who He is. Someone might say, "But I don't like that part of God." Our response has to be, "Well, adjust."

We have to adjust. Do you know why? Because God says, "I, the LORD, do not change" (Mal. 3:6). Have you ever had to tell your children that if they want to live in your house, they have to adjust to your methods? This is God's universe. It is His house, and we need to adjust to His rules.

Romans 1:18 teaches there is no time when God is not reacting to sin. The problem is that people "suppress [hold down] the truth in unrighteousness." People don't want to deal with the truth.

But we have to tell the truth and point out that God's holy indignation reacts against sin every time and everywhere it shows up. The verb in verse 18 is a present tense, meaning God's wrath "keeps on being revealed" against sin.

We can go all the way back to the beginning of biblical history and see this principle in action. When Adam and Eve disobeyed God, they got booted out of the Garden. Then the whole world resisted God in the days of Noah, and God destroyed the world with a flood. People got together again in Genesis 11 to build a monument to man at Babel. The Bible says God's wrath was kindled, and He came down and destroyed their program.

The cities of Sodom and Gomorrah are nowhere to be found today because they were judged by the fierce wrath of God.

Pharaoh told Moses he was not going to let the children of Israel go. Ten times God demonstrated His wrath to the

Egyptians. But Pharaoh still didn't get the message, so he and his army drowned in the sea.

Korah rebelled against Moses, and Moses said, "Everyone on God's side stand over here. Everyone on Korah's side stand over there." After the people decided whose side they were on, the Bible says that the earth opened up. God, in His wrath, commanded the earth to swallow Korah and all his followers.

Even Jesus couldn't bypass the wrath of God when our sins were placed on Him at the cross. There, God unleashed the fury of eternal wrath on His eternal Son as He bore the sins of the world. If not even God's sinless Son escaped His wrath, we'd better take this seriously. Don't mess with this. Psalm 7:11 teaches that "God is angry with the wicked every day" (KJV). Every time we think an evil thought or do an evil deed, God's anger is kindled because He is so perfect that He must react to unrighteousness. Looking at Romans 1, where Paul explains why God reveals His wrath against the unrighteousness of men, helps us to understand why:

> Because that which is known about God is evident within them; for God made it evident to them. For since the creation of the world His invisible attributes, His eternal power and divine nature, have been clearly seen, being understood through what has been made, so that they are without excuse. (vv. 19–20)

While we can't see God's essence, we can see God's effect, just like we see the wind's effect. Between the truth God put within us and what is evident all around us, we are left without excuse. God has made His reality crystal clear. That's why no matter where you go in the world, you will find people worshiping something.

Our problem is not evolution, it is devolution. Evolution says that man started small and grew great. But the truth is that man has devolved. Man started great but grew smaller spiritually and morally. Why? Because even though people knew God, "they did not honor Him as God, or give thanks; but they became futile in their speculations, and their foolish heart was darkened" (Rom. 1:21).

Paul says we didn't treat God like He was God. If Paul were to visit our churches today, he would likely ask, "How in the world can you come here on a Sunday morning and claim to worship God as God and then ignore Him all week long? That's backwards. The human race has been contaminated by this thing called sin and therefore deserves God's wrath."

The problem gets worse in verse 23, which says, "[They] exchanged the glory of the incorruptible God for an image in the form of corruptible man and of birds and four-footed animals and crawling creatures"—and of cars and of houses and of money and of clothes and on and on. God has been exchanged. We have taken Him back like a Christmas present that doesn't fit, and we have said, "We want our money back." Rather than glorifying God as the great God He is, people have elevated everything but God to His place.

So what does God do with people like that? It is stated three times in the remaining verses of Romans 1 (vv. 24, 26, 28). He gives up on those who insist on perverting the knowledge of Him. That means He unleashes and releases these people to fulfill their wildest dreams and enjoy the consequences thereof.

The wrath of God in history is seen when God takes His hand of restraint off and says, "You want it, you've got it" without Him.

He lets them enjoy the fruit of what they want so badly. He says, "You want independence from Me? You've got it. You want to live your own life? You've got it. You want to be your own god? You've got it—and everything that comes with it."

Romans 1:24 says, "God gave them over in the lusts of their hearts to impurity." He also gave them up to "degrading passions" (v. 26). We see a "devolution" here. First God gave them up to general lusts to fulfill the desires of their hearts. Then the lusts begin to take specific shape because now humans come up with wild stuff and all kinds of degrading evil.

What kind of stuff? "Women exchanged the natural function for that which is unnatural" (v. 26). Similarly, "And in the same way also the men abandoned the natural function of the woman and burned in their desire toward one another, men with men committing indecent acts and receiving in their own persons the due penalty of their error" (v. 27). That is homosexuality.

We have come up with all manner of sin and with it, the emotional and physical consequences that devastate us today. In the righteous revelation of His wrath, God withdraws His restraint against sin and its consequences, and evil begins to spread. New diseases show up. Crime increases. Respect for life deteriorates. Life loses its value. Families are destroyed.

But we still haven't hit bottom. We have not arrived at the worst stage yet. Stage one is what I called above "general passions," a do-your-own-thing approach. But then people go wild and devise insane ways to satisfy their lusts: that is stage two. Then they get so used to what they are doing that they wind up at stage three. Verse 28 says, "And just as they did not see fit to acknowledge God any longer, God gave them over to a depraved mind, to do those things which are not proper."

God will let people get so crazy in their sin that they can no longer think right, perceive right, or act right. They go stark-raving mad spiritually, morally, physically, ethically, and every other way. This madness shows itself in so many horrible ways that Paul merely needs to list them and we get the message (vv. 28–32). These degradations don't need to be illustrated.

Given what happens in this country in an average twenty-four hour span, it is interesting to see that breakdown in society, murder, and rebellion against parents show up in sin's "Hall of Shame." But even these aren't the lowest man can go. The real kicker comes in verse 32, the capstone of this section: "And although they know the ordinance of God, that those who practice such things are worthy of death, they not only do the same, but also give hearty approval to those who practice them."

You know you've hit bottom in God's wrath when people do insane things and other people seek to legitimize, legalize, and be entertained by them. When it gets this bad, it doesn't matter who's on the school board, the city council, or even in the White House. When the wrath of God is your problem, the mercy of God is your only solution.

How can people deny and pervert the truth of God this badly? Because they don't like the God of Romans 1. They want a God who looks and acts like them, who says, "Well, I understand. You know, everybody sins." But the God of the Bible presents the greatest possible threat to their sinful lives. This God reveals His wrath against unrighteousness wherever it is found. We see God's wrath executing His justice in history right now, but this is not the end of it. The wrath of God will continue in eternity:

> But because of your stubbornness and unrepentant heart
> you are storing up wrath for yourself in the day of wrath and
> revelation of the righteous judgment of God. (Rom. 2:5)

Sometimes we get upset because evil people seem to keep getting away with evil. No, their sin account keeps growing. Many people will never have much trouble in this life. But if you could only see the bill awaiting them in eternity. The psalmist pictured the wrath of God like a bow being drawn back (Ps. 7:12). The more sinners sin, while refusing to repent, the farther God pulls back the bow.

You know the farther a bowman pulls back the arrow, the harder it will hit and the deeper it will penetrate. God says that when He lets His arrow go, it is going to penetrate the unrighteous with great agony. That is why the Bible cautions us not to become envious of the wicked. Never get all upset because bad folks have it good and good folks have it bad down here. God just hasn't let His arrow go yet.

Evil people are storing up God's wrath, and the Bible says that God will let His arrow fly at the judgment. This will usher in eternity, which will mean hell for those under His wrath. Hell is not a popular subject. I would prefer that it not be part of the deal, but I'm not making the rules. And God has said there is a place where those who reject Him will be punished forever.

This doctrine is so critical that John the Baptist warned, "flee from the wrath to come" (Matt. 3:7). Jesus said that in hell, "their worm does not die" (Mark 9:48). In other words, there is no death there, no time when the conscience is at ease. Hell is a place of desolation and great pain as a result of being separated from God.

In Revelation 20:10–15, John describes the great and final judgment when Satan and those who reject Christ will be thrown in the "lake of fire" along with "death and Hades" (the abode of the dead, a "holding tank" for those awaiting judgment). The lake of fire is eternal punishment, for its inhabitants "will be tormented day and night forever and ever" (v. 10).

That isn't a pleasant picture, and many people deal with it simply by saying, "I don't believe that." You'd better be sure, because no one can afford to be wrong about this one. If you miss this one, you'll get a bill that can never, ever be paid.

The Bible's most descriptive story about eternal punishment isn't designed to make us feel good. But when you have life-threatening cancer and need radical treatment, making you feel good is not the doctor's first goal. Sin is a cancer, and God's eternal wrath will be the outcome of it unless we have radical surgery to remove it.

The story I'm referring to is found in Luke 16:19–31, and since it fell from the lips of Jesus, we need to give it careful attention. It is the account of the rich man and Lazarus. When both men die, Jesus peels back the corners of eternity and gives us a look at both sides. Lazarus was carried by angels who put him in Abraham's bosom, what we would call paradise or heaven.

The rich man, called Dives by tradition, went to Hades (v. 23), the abode of the evil dead, as I mentioned above. But first, Jesus noted his burial in verse 22. I am sure they had a big funeral for this guy. I bet the limousines were all lined up out front, with a police escort waiting to lead the procession down the middle of Main Street.

At the funeral, they had to cut the eulogies short, because so many people wanted to talk about how much money Dives had given to charity and how nice he was and what a great credit he was to the community. But the rich man couldn't enjoy all that, because he was in "agony" in the flames (v. 24). That means he could feel.

He could see, too. Jesus says that Dives looked up "and saw Abraham far away, and Lazarus in his bosom" (v. 23). He saw what he was missing. The great tragedy of hell is not only what you are going through, but what you could have had and are missing. This definitely exposes the notion that hell is where the party is. God throws the party in heaven.

Dives then asked Abraham to send Lazarus with just a finger full of water to ease his pain. You would have thought he would ask for a bucket of water or even a whole lake, but he didn't. He wanted a finger's worth of water. Whenever you feel like one drop of water will change your existence, you are in bad shape.

But Abraham answered, "I'm sorry. A great gulf is fixed between us and you. We can't come over there and you can't come over here" (see vv. 25–26).

Do you know the worst part of hell? It will be the eternal torment of remembering that on such and such a day, the person sat in church, heard that preacher say this place was real, and didn't do anything about it. Hell is knowing that you could have addressed the issue of your eternal destiny, but never did.

You didn't take seriously the wrath of God.

No help came for Dives. He remained fully conscious. He had his memory, his conscience, and all of his physical senses intact, but all he experienced was agony. Hell had no fellowship. God will eternally quarantine all those who are not rightly related to Him so they won't mess up the enjoyment of heaven for those who are rightly related to Him.

The Bible does teach that hell has degrees of punishment. Jesus says those who knew more will be worse off than those who knew less (Luke 12:47–48). In other words, a person who rejects Christ at our church where I pastor in Dallas is going to be more severely punished than someone who has not had the same opportunities. The second person may have rejected God, but he or she did so with far less information.

But even though hell has degrees of punishment, I don't want even the slightest of those degrees. Have you ever thought about how long eternity is? It will keep you awake at night.

A tombstone in an old cemetery reads,

Pause stranger when you pass me by.
As you are now, so once was I.
As I am now, so you will be
So prepare for death and follow me.

Someone came by one day and read the inscription, then picked up some chalk and wrote underneath it,

To follow you, I am not content.
Until I know which way you went.

You should know who you are following because the issue is your eternal destiny. Don't follow your relatives to hell. Don't follow your friends to eternal torment. Don't let people lead you down the path to eternal destruction, because God is a God of wrath, His righteous retribution against sin.

Keep in mind, though, God does not just come out of nowhere and lower the boom on unsuspecting people who had no chance to do anything about their eternal destinies. In his discussion of God's sovereignty, Paul points out that God endures "with much patience" even those people who are "vessels of wrath prepared for destruction" (Rom. 9:22), people we might call hell-bent.

As we saw earlier, God is long-suffering. "The Lord . . . is patient toward you, not wishing for any to perish but for all to come to repentance" (2 Peter 3:9). God is not wrathful because He wants to injure. He is wrathful because He is just. That is what we have to understand. His sense of justice demands that He react to sin.

But God's wrath is preceded by so much patience. Remember that for years He put up with a rebellious world before sending the flood? God's patience lasts a lifetime. He waits on us, forgives us, not giving us what we deserve, and holds back His wrath toward us. He says, "Come to Me now." But we keep putting Him off by not submitting and turning to Christ.

We say, "Not now. Tomorrow. Before I die." Then the clock runs out. I don't know how old you are, but I know that youth is relative when it comes to facing God's wrath. You can measure how young you are only against your death date, not your birthdate. A person who is going to die at the age of twenty-five is old at fifteen. But if that same person lives to be ninety, he or she is still young at fifty.

No one knows their death date, which is why today is always the day of salvation (Heb. 4:7–15). Don't put salvation off. Put something else off, but not this. God is patient, so come to Him while you can.

How patient is God? Numbers 14 tells about the unbelief of Israel when the people refused to believe God and take the Promised Land. God was angry. He wanted to destroy those rebels and start over with Moses (vv. 11–12). But Moses reminded God of His patience, and He granted the nation a stay of execution, so to speak (vv. 18–20).

But read the rest of Numbers 14, and you will see that God did judge His people. Too many make the mistake described in Ecclesiastes 8:11, which says that people take God's delay in judging sin as an excuse to sin more. They figure they are home free. They think God has slackened (2 Peter 3:9). So instead of saying, "God has been patient with me, I had better repent!" they say, "God is so easygoing that He is not really going to do anything."

Hebrews 9:27 says, "it is appointed for men to die once and after this comes judgment." Not a second chance, not a lot of slack, not a reprieve, but judgment. Romans 2:4 says it this way: "Or do you think lightly of the riches of His kindness and tolerance and patience, not knowing that the kindness of God leads you to repentance?" If He hasn't judged you yet, you should be running to Him in gratitude and repentance.

The Bible pictures the unsaved as dangling over hell. In Luke 13:1–5, Jesus makes clear that the unsaved are just one heartbeat, one act of violence, or one accident away from God's judgment. His examples show that the blow could fall at any moment. The lost are being held only by the grace of God, and when He releases His grip, they are gone. It doesn't matter how young or healthy they are. When God lets go, they're gone. But the Bible also tells us of an escape.

A choice must be made. Individuals go to hell by his or her choice, not because God is mean. The Bible says God made hell for Satan and his angels, not for people. His justice demands payment for sin, but in His mercy, He provided a substitute to take our punishment for us. This is good news! God's system of justice allows for a substitute.

There once was a king who ruled over a very wicked people. So he made a law that said, "Anyone who violates the law will have both eyes put out." The first young man to violate the law was brought to the king for judgment—but when the king looked up he cried out in anguish, because it was his son.

This king faced a dilemma. Justice demanded that he put his son's eyes out. But his love said, "This is my son. I can't put my son's eyes out." How did he balance justice and love? The king put out one of his son's eyes and one of his own eyes. So whoever saw the two of them together saw justice and love in operation: justice, because two eyes were put out as the law demanded; and love, because the king loved his son enough to give his eye for him.

That is a good illustration, but God went one step further. Jesus paid it all. He took all of our sins, rebellion, and guilt, and paid for them all on Calvary. It cost Him His life, not just an eye. Jesus paid it all.

That is why God will not tolerate people rejecting Christ. He will not tolerate it because an eternal God let His eternal Son pay an eternal price for our eternal sin that eternal people might live with Him eternally. But if we reject the God who paid the price and bore the wrath of God due us through His Son for our sin, then we will face the eternal consequences.

God paid too high a price for us to play games with His wrath. He said, "I'm telling you in advance, I'm a wrathful God. But I'm going to do something Myself to satisfy My wrath, because nothing you could do could ever satisfy Me. My Son will become a man like you, except without sin, so I can forgive you of your sin. But once My Son does this, and I raise Him from the dead to let you know this is real, don't mess with Me! Take Me very seriously. Don't presume on My goodness."

That's why 1 Thessalonians 1:10 says "Jesus, who rescues us from the wrath to come." According to Romans 5:8–9,

> God demonstrates His own love toward us, in that while we were yet sinners, Christ died for us. Much more then, having now been justified by His blood, we shall be saved from the wrath of God through Him.

You are saved from the wrath of God through Christ, not by attending church, being a nice person, or doing good in the community. You will be saved from the wrath to come only by the eternal provision of Jesus Christ. You must put faith alone in Christ alone for the forgiveness of sin and the gift of eternal life.

You say, "But I'm already a Christian. I'm already saved. None of this applies to me."

True, if you are a Christian, you will never experience the

eternal wrath of God. You may undergo His discipline for sin, but you will never face His wrath. This is why God offers us the opportunity to limit, or even reverse, some or all of the consequences of our sin through confession and repentance (2 Cor. 7:9). Repentance is the internal decision and determination to turn from sin to God in order to be restored to fellowship with God. True repentance is validated through the visible manifestation of its fruits (Matt. 3:8). Believers will be delivered from God's wrath against sin in history as they take advantage of the spiritual provisions of the resurrected Christ (Rom. 5:10).

But this message about God's eternal wrath does apply to you if you've got a brother, sister, aunt, uncle, or anyone else who does not know Jesus Christ. You can't just let the person die without Jesus Christ, without hearing from your mouth the need to flee from the wrath to come.

You don't want your family, friends, and coworkers going to a lost eternity, saying, "But I worked next to her for twenty years and she never told me about this. I was his relative, we went to family reunions together every year, and he never warned me about hell. I lived next door to the man, and he never said anything to me about this."

The wrath of God applies to you if there will be people in hell you and I knew and loved and worked beside, but who never heard how they could flee His wrath because we never opened our mouths to be a witness. Our job is to tell a lost world about Jesus Christ so their blood won't be on our hands (Ezek. 3:15–19).

I don't want to stand before Jesus and have Him look at me and say, "Where are all your friends? Where is your family? They are not here because you didn't tell them. You were scared to witness. But you weren't scared to talk about everything else. Why was I too big a problem to talk about?"

A pastor who wanted his congregation to understand that people were dying and going to hell got up one Sunday morning and said, "It bothers me that you people aren't sharing your faith. And millions are dying and going to hell. You don't give a [expletive]."

Then he said, "Right now, most of you are more concerned that I used that word than that millions of people are dying and going to hell. You are upset about that when it ought to be setting your feet afire that you've got relatives and neighbors and coworkers to call this afternoon and tell about Jesus."

I don't recommend this pastor's method, but we need to get our priorities straight. So I have two messages. If you are a Christian, you'd better start talking because people could lose out on this gift of mercy if you keep quiet. If you are not a Christian, you'd better run to Jesus today because He is offering you a pardon, and the clock is ticking.

In 1829, a Philadelphia man named George Wilson robbed the US mail post office and killed someone in the process. Wilson was arrested, brought to trial, convicted, and sentenced to be hanged. Some friends intervened on his behalf and were finally able to obtain a pardon for Wilson from President Andrew Jackson.

But when informed of this, Wilson refused to accept the pardon. The sheriff was unwilling to carry out the sentence. How could he hang a pardoned man? An appeal was sent to President Jackson. Perplexed, Jackson turned to the US Supreme Court to decide the case. Chief Justice John Marshall ruled that a pardon rejected is no pardon at all. George Wilson would have to face his sentence. Wilson was hanged, although his pardon lay on the sheriff's desk.

God forbid that, at the judgment, He should ever have to say that we did not receive the pardon for sin through the salvation of Jesus Christ—about us or anyone we care about. We need to warn people to escape God's wrath and embrace the forgiveness He freely offers to all who will come by faith to Him to receive it.

Chapter 5

THE SOVEREIGNTY OF GOD

One of God's chief theological attributes is His sovereignty. Sovereignty simply refers to His rule over all creation. According to Ephesians 1:11, He does all things after the counsel of His own will. In Romans 11:36 we read, "For from him and through him and for him are all things" (NIV).

Absolutely nothing escapes His rule and influence. God is in charge of all things because He has created and sustains all things. Within God's sovereignty, though, is another key reality concerning God that is often overlooked, blamed, and misunderstood. This involves His providence. The providence of God includes the miraculous and mysterious ways in which He intersects and interconnects things in order to bring about His sovereignty.

God's sovereignty is what He wants to happen. God's providence is where He establishes things and connects them so that His sovereignty does happen.

The reason we often misunderstand things in the area of providence is because without a full awareness of where things are headed (sovereignty), we might wonder about God's providential choices along the way. It is only when you understand the link between providence and sovereignty that you will become conscious of the wisdom of God's work in our world and in your life.

God *is* sovereign, yes. But because He has granted freedom to us as human beings, He has to incorporate providential involvement in order to achieve His sovereignty. He will not allow our freedom to thwart His purposes, so He must stitch the freedom of humanity into His plans in such a way as to create a tapestry called destiny. This includes even using—though not condoning—sin, sinners, and Satan to accomplish His sovereign purposes, a theological construct called theodicy, which we will look at later.

Both the sovereignty and providence of God are such critical spiritual truths that knowing and living by them can radically transform your life. When you are able to discern how God sovereignly and providentially works in history, as well as in the present, you are able to move along life's journey with a purpose and intention that will propel you forward.

Let's start with sovereignty. God's sovereignty concerns His absolute rule and control over all of His creation. God rules completely as He sits on the throne of the universe as Lord. Everything that happens comes about because He either directly causes it or consciously allows it. Nothing enters into history or could ever exist outside of history that does not come under the complete control of God. Thus, with God, there is no such thing as luck, chance, happenstance, or fate.

Only when you understand that this is the kind of God with whom we engage will you take seriously the issue of His authority. The sovereignty of God means that He exercises His prerogative to do whatever He pleases with His creation. God can do whatever He wants to do with creation simply because it all is His (see Ps. 115:3).

I understand that most people don't want God to do whatever He wants because they want to do whatever they want. What people want today is a God who will pop up conveniently when they want or need Him, and then when they are finished with Him, go away. Similar to a jack-in-the-box, people want a God-in-the-box who will bless, forgive, encourage, love, and direct them when they spin the wheel. But they want Him to disappear when their thoughts and decisions return to their own wills.

But let's get this straight: nothing exists outside the rule of God in your life, in this world, or in creation. Scripture says that not one bird falls to the ground of which He is not fully aware and that not one hair on a person's head is lost that He is not fully overseeing (Matt. 10:29, Luke 12:7). God's sovereignty stretches beyond the limits of life itself. He is sovereign in the big things and small. He rules over all.

The Bible provides ample insight into God's sovereign rule. We read:

"But He is unique and who can turn Him? And what His soul desires, that He does." (Job 23:13)

"I know that You can do all things, and that no purpose of Yours can be thwarted." (Job 42:2)

But our God is in the heavens; He does whatever He pleases. (Ps. 115:3)

Whatever the LORD pleases, He does, in heaven and in earth, in the seas and in all deeps. (Ps. 135:6)

The LORD has made everything for its own purpose, even the wicked for the day of evil. (Prov. 16:4)

"Even from eternity I am He, and there is none who can deliver out of My hand; I act and who can reverse it?" (Isa. 43:13)

"The One forming light and creating darkness, causing well-being and creating calamity; I am the LORD who does all these." (Isa. 45:7)

Also we have obtained an inheritance, having been predestined according to His purpose who works all things after the counsel of His will. (Eph. 1:11)

For from Him and through Him and to Him are all things. To Him be the glory forever. Amen. (Rom. 11:36)

"Then I heard something like the voice of a great multitude and like the sound of many waters and like the sound of mighty peals of thunder, saying, 'Hallelujah! For the Lord our God, the Almighty, reigns.'" (Rev. 19:6)

God rules! Even when it looks like He's not ruling, He's ruling. When chaos appears, He's ruling the chaos. When things are falling apart, He's ruling the falling apart of those things.

When we speak of or study God, we are talking of the One who is the absolute Ruler, Owner, Creator, Controller, and Sustainer of all things. Nothing sits outside of His governance. Psalm 24:1 puts it this way, "The earth is the LORD's, and all it contains, the world, and those who dwell in it." By virtue of His ownership, God can do whatever He wants to do whenever He wants to do it.

When you start making universes, creating planets, giving and sustaining life, perhaps then you can start dictating how God ought to run His universe. But until and unless you get that divine clout, you cannot exercise that divine prerogative. The prerogative always belongs to God, never to us, and He does whatever He chooses.

Perhaps you can relate to this concept better if I illustrate it through a home. If you own a home, you are responsible for your home. Suppose someone came to your home and started telling you what to change or do differently? What if someone came in and started rearranging your furniture?

Our son Anthony had flown in for some work he had to do in Dallas and decided to stay in our home. Last I had checked, Anthony had not paid our electric bill, water bill, or house note and insurance. But somehow he must have gotten confused and thought he had. I say that because while I was nearly ready for bed, Anthony walked into my bedroom where the thermostat was located and turned it down. Not only that, he walked in without knocking, complaining that he was hot. Apparently,

Anthony likes to keep his living area extra-cold because it feels fine to him.

But as far as I was concerned, Anthony was a visitor and not an owner. So I let him know he could sleep in the den and use the separate unit for that area in order to keep it as cool as he wanted in there. But in my home, and in my bedroom, we were not going to keep it cold! In other words, he had come into my home functioning like a sovereign while being only a guest. That didn't make me feel that great.

Yet how do you think God feels as the owner of this world when He has grown kids wanting to dictate to Him His own creation?

THE PURPOSE OF GLORY

The sovereignty of God means first that He exercises His prerogative to do with His creation whatever He chooses. Consider 1 Corinthians 8:6, which says,

> For us there is but one God, the Father, from whom are all things and we exist for Him; and one Lord, Jesus Christ, by whom are all things, and we exist through Him.

You exist for God. That is why you were created. You were not made just to get a good job, get married, have kids, and live happily ever after. Those you call blessings and gifts. You were created to bring God glory and to accomplish His purposes on earth. That's why you will find no rest in life until you find your rest in Him.

The sovereignty of God involves the exercise of His attributes in order to maintain His glory and accomplish His will.

One might mention at this point the question of the origin of evil. Since God is sovereign, why did He allow the existence and proliferation of evil, especially in light of the fact that God hates sin (Rom. 1:18), is completely holy (Isa. 6:3), and cannot sin (Ps. 5:4; 1 John 1:5) or tempt others to do so (James 1:13)? On top of all that, He has the power to destroy Satan, the spiritual architect of evil. Theologians have pondered this question for ages, and as I mentioned earlier, theodicy is the summation of that ongoing pondering.

First, since God does everything for His greatest glory (Eph. 1:11–12), we must naturally conclude that God will get more glory with the existence of sin than without it. While God does not need sin to exist nor is sin necessary, He can still use the existence of sin as a backdrop to His glory.

This makes sense because some of God's attributes are most clearly demonstrated against the backdrop of sin. The greatness of His love shows most clearly in contrast to our sinfulness (Rom. 5:8). God's holiness and wrath, two indispensable aspects of His nature, could never be fully seen without the reality of sin (Rom. 1:18; 9:22–23). Most important, the magnificence of His grace could hardly be measured except against the ugliness of sin (Eph. 2:1–7). Thus, in allowing sin, the glory of God's attributes and character is most visibly displayed.

Second, in allowing the existence of evil, God is allowing everything that can be attempted to thwart His kingdom so that throughout the ages to come, it will be unquestionably clear that no enemy or scheme can succeed against the Almighty

One. When this is over, no one is ever again going to come up with the dumb idea of rebelling against His authority, for history will demonstrate that every attempt has been tried and none has been successful. This comprehensive defeat of evil will be a primary basis for God's people giving Him praise (Rev. 19:1–6).

In addition, when God created His world, He included something in His creation called *choice*. He gave us freedom to make our own decisions. If He would have removed choice, then He would have removed one of the primary purposes of humanity because He wanted us to respond to Him by choice, not by mandate. Thus, when He put Adam and Eve in the garden, He also put trees in the garden. He told them they could eat of all the trees except for one. They got to choose. And they chose poorly.

Bear in mind that choice never negates sovereignty. The best way I know how to illustrate this involves the game of football. On a football field, you have sovereign lines that are non-negotiable. These include sidelines, goal lines, hash lines, and yard lines. The lines don't move. They exist as non-negotiable boundaries. However, within those boundaries each team can change what they do. They can choose which plays they run or don't run. They can change whether they run or pass the ball. They get to make a lot of choices, but what they don't get to do is change the boundaries because the boundaries are fixed.

God has established sovereign boundaries that He will let nobody cross. Yet within these boundaries of His sovereignty, He allows each of us to make choices. If and when you make the right choice, you move forward. If and when you make a poor choice, you get penalized or the opposition overcomes you and you move backwards. You lose yardage in life. God Himself will determine when you have gone too far and infringed on His sovereign control. He will also determine the consequences or whether He will show mercy.

The freedom of choice allows for the presence of evil. God didn't create evil, but He did create choice. And that choice opens the door for the possibility of evil, but mankind makes evil actual. In His providence, God allows things even if they are against Him because those things He allows that are against Him create the opportunity for Him to manifest and display attributes about Himself that would otherwise not be seen. While the choice of sin may open the door for God to reveal His wrath, it also opens the door for Him to reveal His mercy and redemptive powers. Everything that happens reveals another aspect of God—whether it appears to be happening for or against Him. He's going to show up. God will always accomplish His purpose. What you do, or do not do, will never block God from getting to where He has designed to go. He will go with you, around you, or over you, but you will never interfere with His end result. God will always accomplish His purposes because God never limits Himself to one path.

Finally, God allows evil because of His love. He does not wish to coerce obedience. For God to coerce obedience would invalidate the authentic nature of that obedience, especially since God looks at the heart (Rom. 8:27), which remains disobedient. In order for people to function authentically as God's image-bearers, which includes functioning as moral agents with the power to choose, the possibility of evil must exist. For God to have negated that possibility would be for Him to nullify the very thing He created. Personhood would be reduced to robotics.

We must, therefore, conclude that God neither causes, incites, authorizes, or approves of sin. He does, however, permit it by allowing His creatures, whom He has endowed with a moral will, to rebel against His authority. He then sovereignly overrules their evil to accomplish His sovereign predetermined purposes. In the allowance of evil, God demonstrates how great He really is. Or as Joseph so accurately articulated when giving his analysis of the evil done to him by his brothers who sold him into slavery, "you meant evil against me, but God meant it for good in order to bring about this present result, to preserve many people alive" (Gen. 50:20).

GOD CAUSES

One of the most-referenced Scriptures on the attribute of God's sovereignty is Romans 8:28. It's a favorite verse of many people, and you may even know it by heart. It is a powerful verse because it brings to light this issue of sovereignty and also of providence. It says,

> And we know that God causes all things to work together for good to those who love God, to those who are called according to His purpose.

The key word in this passage is "causes." God's position as Supreme Ruler over all that He has created gives Him the opportunity and responsibility to *cause* whatever He wants to cause. No matter how difficult the journey, no matter how challenging the trip, and no matter how precarious the pathways, providence means God caused it for a greater purpose.

You have probably heard of the city Providence, Rhode Island. This city was named Providence as the colonies were being established. The pilgrims felt that God had overseen the events leading them to their safe arrival as well as the provisions that were made for them when they landed. Thus, they attached God's sovereign intervention to the name of where they chose to reside. It would serve as a constant reminder that despite how things may have once appeared, He had a destination He had been taking them to all along.

Providence is God's governance of all events, which means by exclusion that there is really no such thing as luck, chance, or happenstance. There is nothing left to fate at all. Romans 8:28 doesn't say that God causes some things to work together. Rather, it says He causes them *all*.

And while the pilgrims may have named their town of Providence rightly, not all of our founding fathers had an accurate understanding of God's sovereign hand. A good number of them were "deists." Deists are people who believe in a God who created everything but then left it alone to run itself. This is like winding up a clock and then letting that wind work its way out on its own. In a sense, a deist believes that God has abandoned His creation to churn its way through the natural laws He established. Thus, God is a long-distance God to them. He is not eminently involved in day-to-day life.

Yet the attribute of sovereignty argues that God has not abandoned the world, but rather works within His creation to *cause* everything to conform to His ultimate unchangeable will. In fact, Colossians 1:17 says clearly, "He is before all things, and in Him all things hold together." Not only does He hold everything together, He holds us together too. Acts 17 records,

> "The God who made the world and all things in it, since He is Lord of heaven and earth, does not dwell in temples made with hands; nor is He served by human hands, as though He needed anything, since He Himself gives to all people life and breath and all things." (vv. 24–25)

Everything you and I have, or possess, has been given to us as a direct result of God choosing to do so. There is nothing that you have received that was not created either by God or by things that God created. You might want to read that sentence again, or underline it. It's important. God produces each and every single thing. Because He does, He claims sovereignty over it all as well. He controls it. He is the consummate, ultimate micromanager. He is intricately, intimately involved in every single detail. He manages the universe and all of us in it to the highest degree possible. And if He weren't, if He would just take a moment to step back and not hold the universe in place, we all would be obliterated in an instant.

From His vantage point, it all makes perfect sense. Yet from ours, time can seem marked by an endless array or series of contingencies that we may call "luck" or "chance" or even "random events."

But that is just how it seems; that is not how it is. Because nothing is random with God. He is working out the details of everything, not just watching it transpire. What is more, He is working out the details toward His intended goal. Once you and

I come to understand His overarching goal, we will understand better His pathways.

God's ultimate goal always results in God's glory. Ephesians 1 highlights this for us:

> In love He predestined us to adoption as sons through Jesus Christ to Himself, according to the kind intention of His will, to the praise of the glory of His grace. . . . to the end that we who were the first to hope in Christ would be to the praise of His glory. . . . with a view to the redemption of God's own possession, to the praise of His glory." (vv. 4–6, 12, 14)

The primary reason God is working everything out toward His intended outcome is "to the praise of His glory." God sets out to guarantee all that He has created fulfills and satisfies its created purpose, which brings glory back to Himself.

Like it or not, God exists for His own glory. Now, you can fight that truth, fuss at it, argue it, not want it, reject it, accuse it, or anything else you want to do. But whatever you do about it, it's not going to change it. God exists for God. So does everything He made. He made everything for Himself. We are made for God. Our lives are not about us but about Him and His glory.

Anything that competes with, negates, or downplays God's glory exists in a perpetual state of misalignment. It is out of order. God made *all* things to display His attributes, character, and power.

There is another reason, though, why God causes all things to work together. He does it for His glory, yes, but He also does it for us, for good. Romans 8:28 says God "causes all things to work together for good." He is bringing about our benefit. The word "good" means that which is beneficial. Thus, God is also seeking to bring about benefits and blessings in our own lives as well, in the lives of those who love Him and walk according to the paths of His purpose.

Please don't misread that verse to make it apply to everyone, everywhere. Too many people do that. It does not say that God causes all things in every single way to work out for good. No, it specifically refers to those who love Him and are called according to His purpose. There is bad in this world. Negative things do happen. The assumption is that when they do, as we discussed earlier, God Himself must not be good. But the presence of darkness doesn't negate the power of light. Light exists to drive out darkness, not to eliminate it entirely. Romans 8:28 doesn't say that God causes all things to *be* good. Rather, He integrates all things to work together *for* good in the lives of those who love Him and follow His paths. His is the invisible hand operating behind the scenes of the good, bad, and the ugly in life. He maneuvers the many circumstances toward His intended end. And God's ultimate goal for every believer is that they be conformed to the image of His Son in their attitudes and actions, character and conduct (Rom. 8:29).

One of the problems we often face on our life's journeys is that we do not see the end. We get frustrated and feel lost when we can't see where we are headed. Have you ever felt frustrated when you were driving and you got lost? Or have you been with someone who got frustrated when they were driving and got lost? Yet when a map was found, or a GPS, or directions from a stranger that pointed the way, the frustrations fell away. This is because reaching the end came into sight.

What happens to us, though, in following God along the pathways of His sovereignty is that He does not always give us the directions to the very end. He does not provide us with the full map view so we can see every turn we will eventually take. He gives us a glimpse here, or a direction there, but rarely the entire picture. Thus, people often live in a perpetual state of frustration, not knowing how each step, each day, each set of circumstances or conversations are leading to the right place. Without a full view of providence tied to a surrender to sovereignty, these frustrations can mount into an overwhelming cascade of emotions threatening you like an avalanche on a blizzardy day.

Be assured, nothing comes to any of us that doesn't pass through God's providential fingers first. You have to know that. You have to believe that. You have to trust that. You have to rest in that. That mindset will situate you so that you can respond to life's challenges, setbacks, and randomness with a spirit of intentionality and persevering faith.

When you recognize the idiosyncratic elements of the invisible yet sovereign hand of God, you will discover the details and direction leading you to your destiny.

Our God is sovereign. That means there is no such thing as luck. The word ought to be expunged from the dictionary, or at least from any serious usage. You are never lucky or unlucky. Under God, no chance happenings occur. Anything that happens to you, good or bad, must pass through His fingers first. There are no accidents with God. God never says, "Oops, I didn't see that one coming."

I like the story of the cowboy who applied for health insurance. The agent routinely asked him, "Have you ever had any accidents?"

The cowboy replied, "Well no, I've not had any accidents. I was bitten by a rattlesnake once, and a horse did kick me in the ribs. That laid me up for a while, but I haven't had any accidents."

The agent said, "Wait a minute. I'm confused. A rattlesnake bit you, and a horse kicked you. Weren't those accidents?"

"No, they did that on purpose."

That cowboy had the right idea. Things don't just happen. Everything that occurs, occurs under the hand of a sovereign God. Once you understand that, all of life takes on a different shape and perspective. In a universe controlled by a sovereign God, there can be no chance happenings, no luck, no mistakes; good and bad fall under His control.

A great example of this comes in Exodus 4, where Moses tried to tell God, "I can't talk. I stutter." Look at God's answer in verse 11: "Who has made man's mouth? Or who makes him dumb or deaf, or seeing or blind? Is it not I, the Lord?" God knew all about Moses's speech impediment. God gave it to him.

Another great biblical example of sovereignty is found in Daniel 4. This is an often overlooked but powerful chapter because sometimes we get a big head and have lessons to learn from it. A song from 1971 began, "Mr. Big Stuff, just who do you think you are?"[2] Well, King Nebuchadnezzar thought he was God's gift to creation. He thought he was Mr. Big Stuff.

According to verses 29–30, he was walking on the roof of

2. "Mr. Big Stuff," written by Joe Broussard, Carol Washington, and Ralph Williams; performed by Jean Knight (Stax Records, 1971).

his royal palace in Babylon when he looked around and said, "Is this not Babylon the great, which I myself have built as a royal residence by the might of my power and for the glory of my majesty?" Nebuchadnezzar was saying, "I am the man!"

The only problem with verse 30 is that verse 31 follows: "While the word was in the king's mouth, a voice came from heaven, saying, 'King Nebuchadnezzar, to you it is declared: sovereignty has been removed from you.'"

God goes on to say, "You will go insane. You will live with animals, crawl on the ground like an animal, and eat grass like an animal for seven years until you recognize Me as Sovereign of the universe." That prophecy was fulfilled immediately (see verse 33). Nebuchadnezzar went insane, looking and living like a beast. He lost his mind because he forgot who he was.

Seven years later, Nebuchadnezzar came to himself: "But at the end of that period, I, Nebuchadnezzar, raised my eyes toward heaven and my reason returned to me" (v. 34). When did he start to regain his sanity? When he knew where to look. What did he do? "I blessed the Most High and praised and honored Him who lives forever" (v. 34).

Nebuchadnezzar said, "Lord, it's Your dominion. It's Your kingdom." Then he confessed,

"All the inhabitants of the earth [including me] are
    accounted as nothing,
But He does according to His will in the host of heaven
And among the inhabitants of earth;
And no one can ward off His hand
Or say to Him, 'What have You done?'" (v. 35)

Some of us are crazy when it comes to thinking about God, because we think wrong about Him. Until we start thinking right about God, we won't think right about ourselves. Only after Nebuchadnezzar started thinking right about God could he say, "At that time my reason returned to me. And my majesty and splendor were restored to me" (v. 36). Then he summarizes his experience:

> "Now I, Nebuchadnezzar, praise, exalt and honor the King of heaven, for all His works are true and His ways just, and He is able to humble those who walk in pride." (v. 37)

Do you get the point? No matter how high you climb, no matter what name you get, no matter how large your platform, no matter how much money you accumulate, our God is sovereign. That means that while you respect people, no person intimidates you. You give people the honor due them, but you recognize that underneath God, everyone is nothing. Through this painful experience, Nebuchadnezzar came to find out that God doesn't play. He raises up people and brings down people.

While it's legitimate to be grateful that God uses you, believing He uses you because of who you are is illegitimate. Remember, He gave you the gifts, skills, and abilities you have. So He should get the glory that you have the ability to pull off what other people give you credit for.

GOD'S SOVEREIGNTY AND OUR PERSPECTIVE

The sovereignty of God provides us with the proper perspective in which to view all of life. If you understand the sovereignty of God, your life will begin to take shape.

God's sovereignty gives strength and comfort in the midst of life's circumstances (Phil. 4:13). Life is bittersweet. One day you can wake up and be on top of the world. Your job is going well, the money is flowing, your relationships are intact. You just wake up and say, "What a beautiful morning! The people are great! The kids are great! My mother-in-law is great! Everything is great!"

But all that can change in five seconds. Thankfully, when you have a sovereign God, it means that the negative and the positive do not come by chance. The flat tire that made you miss the interview you were banking on to get that job was part of God's sovereign plan. The situation you thought was going to work out a certain way and the job you were sure was yours that was given to someone else were all part of God's sovereign plan.

His sovereignty also means He allows no chance happenings. You can have confidence: "Lord, You did what I thought You weren't going to do. That's because You want to do something else in my life, and I'm excited to see how You are going to use what You just did to do what You want to do. So go ahead and do Your thing, and use it to take me to the next spiritual level of conforming me to the image of Jesus Christ."

When you walk with God, when you live under His control, when you are in His hands, nothing can stifle you. God has allowed the negative, and He's going to use it to propel you. It's not evident at first because we have limited perspective. We're like the boy who was trying to work a puzzle. He couldn't even get two pieces to come together. His father came, and after several minutes, put the whole puzzle together.

The son asked, "Dad, how did you do that?"

"Son, you were looking at the pieces. I saw the whole picture."

It all depends on what you see. From our perspective, we see one piece at a time because we live one day at time. But God sees the whole picture, and He can put the whole thing together. When you understand the sovereignty of God, you believe in the power of prayer because you are convinced of what God can do.

You can't change people. You can't change your mate, but you can get out of the way so God can transform the situation or the person, or even you in it. It is amazing that some people want to quit on things when they have never fasted and prayed over them. If you haven't fasted and prayed, you have not done all that God has called you to do in order to link into His sovereign plan. Jesus says that certain things come only by fasting and praying (see Matt. 17:21).

Certain things you do not get just because you want them and you have done the best you can. Yet other things come only because you have prayed about them to the point of giving up the craving of your appetite to get them.

If I am excited about one doctrine in my own life and ministry, it is God's sovereignty. I do not believe He can give me a vision to do anything that cannot be done as long as it is in His will. Since I have that view, the obstacles seem irrelevant to me. I find the fact that it has never been done before to be irrelevant because the Bible says nothing is impossible with God (Luke 1:37).

The sovereignty of God should lead us to enthusiastic worship of Him. You know what ought to draw us to church on Sunday? The fact that the sovereign God, who holds up the universe by the word of His power, wants to have a meeting with us; that this great God, who gives us the air we breathe every day, who provides us everything we need, wants to meet with us.

When you realize you have a sovereign God, you can't wait to meet with Him. When you have a boss who cares about you and is responsible for your paycheck, you cannot wait to get to work, even if you hate the job, because you know you are not autonomous. If we give our bosses the honor due them for a paycheck, how much more should we give God the honor due Him for the life we have each day? Worship is the proper response to God's sovereignty (Mal. 1:6–11).

First Chronicles 29 brings this out clearly. David was in a building program, and Israel was getting ready to build God a house. David challenged the people to bring their offerings for the temple they would build for God:

> Then the rulers of the fathers' households, and the princes of the tribes of Israel, and the commanders of thousands and of hundreds, with the overseers over the king's work, offered willingly; and for the service for the house of God they gave 5,000 talents and 10,000 darics of gold, and 10,000 talents of silver, and 18,000 talents of brass, and 100,000 talents of iron. (vv. 6–7)

So the people gave generously to the house of God. And as they did so,

> David blessed the LORD in the sight of all the assembly; and David said, "Blessed art Thou, O LORD God of Israel our father, forever and ever. Thine, O LORD, is the greatness and the power and the glory and the victory and the majesty, indeed everything that is in the heavens and the earth; Thine is the dominion, O LORD, and Thou dost exalt Thyself as head over all. Both riches and honor come from Thee, and Thou dost rule over all, and in Thy hand is power and might; and it lies in Thy hand to make great, and to strengthen everyone. Now therefore, our God, we thank Thee, and praise Thy glorious name. (vv. 10–13)

That's what ought to draw you to church on Sunday—to praise God's glorious name, because what king is like our God? Who else can create moons, stars, planets, and other galaxies? Who can create just the right temperature and keep the earth rotating at just the right speed so that it rotates around the sun at just the right season?

Who can give us just the right animals from which we get just the right clothes and the right food? Who can create just the right wood so we can build just the right houses? Who is like our God? He deserves your homage. He deserves your bowing before His face, glorifying His name. He deserves your passionate worship.

If your refrigerator stops one day a week, you call a repairman; it is undependable. If your water alternates between hot and cold, you get it fixed; that is an uncomfortable way to take a shower. If you miss every other mortgage payment, you will be moved out of your house because that is not how a loan works.

What we expect of ourselves and others, should not our sovereign God expect of us, and even more? He wants our dedicated, committed worship. You may say, "But I find it hard to worship God. You don't know what's going on in my life."

You are right. I do not know what is going on in your life, but I know this. It was in the year that King Uzziah died that Isaiah saw the Lord (Isa. 6:1). Maybe your Uzziah is dying. That is, maybe your circumstances are tough because only in the midst of chaos will you take time to look to God. A sovereign God can arrange circumstances to accomplish His purposes. He allows the difficulties and challenges for a reason. Once you begin to believe this truth about His attribute of sovereignty, you will start to see the purpose in the pain. God's endgame for you is good. The direction He is taking you is good. Trust the process. He knows the way.

Chapter 6

THE LOVE OF GOD

A father was having devotions with his family, and they were discussing the love of God. Shortly after devotions, they all sat down to some pancakes and eggs. One kid got only eggs, while the other kid got both pancakes and eggs.

As you can imagine, the kid who got only eggs asked why he did not also get the pancakes. To which the dad replied, "Don't you remember our devotions? Jesus says we are to love like God loves, and that means considering others as more important than ourselves."

The son did not miss a beat when he promptly pointed to his brother and said, "Well, then, you be Jesus!"

It is easy to talk about this concept of love, but it is much harder to live it out. Thankfully, as believers, we have access to God's attribute of love when we abide in Him. Now, don't get me wrong, I'm not referring to an emotion or fuzzy feelings. *Love* has become such a common term that it has lost a lot of its true meaning. After all, we use it for just about anything. I love ice cream. I love chocolate cake. I love chicken. I love that movie. I love your outfit. I loved that sermon. I love this job. We use the word *love* so casually because we often use to merely reflect our emotive connection to something or someone.

But the divine attribute of love has an entirely different meaning altogether. In fact, God does not love, necessarily, as a verb. Rather, He *is* love. First John 4:8 puts it this way: "God is love." In other words, any discussion about love has to start with God because that is who He is. It is not just what He does. It is His self-definition. It is like me saying, "I am Black." It is my racial identity and an unchangeable reality. So when God says He is love, He wants each of us to view love as a defining part of who He is.

Therefore, if you really want to understand the word and how love works, you have to look at God.

GOD HAS ALWAYS LOVED

Now, if this is who God is, then He must have been this forever. God did not become love. Nor did He start loving. In fact, God was love before there was time, space, people, or human emotions. He has always been love, even when nothing existed outside of Himself. Thus, when God first loved—even though there really never was a beginning to His love—He loved Himself.

That may sound self-serving, but keep in mind that God exists as three coequal persons: God the Father, God the Son, and God the Holy Spirit. So when we talk about God, we are not talking about somoene who has never been by Himself. God has never been lonely. He has never been alone. God has never existed in singularity because the doctrine of the Trinity means that one God exists as three persons who are one in essence yet distinct in personality. The Father is not the Son. The Son is not the Spirit. But all three together exists as one Godhead whom we know as the Trinity. Thus, other so-called gods cannot be made the same since no other god can declare love as an intrinsic attribute since they are not triune in nature.

God has always had somebody to love. That's why when the Bible says that God is love. It is telling us that He is operating in a context of love within Himself.

Jesus sought to give insight into this reality, particularly as recorded in John 5:19–20:

> Therefore Jesus answered and was saying to them, "Truly, truly, I say to you, the Son can do nothing of Himself, unless *it is* something He sees the Father doing; for whatever the Father does, these things the Son also does in like manner. For the Father loves the Son, and shows Him all things that He Himself is doing; and *the Father* will show Him greater works than these, so that you will marvel."

Jesus did on earth only what He saw the Father doing. That was, and is, their way of functioning. Jesus' surrender to God's will brings God glory. Similarly, when we surrender to God's will, we also bring Him glory.

Ephesians 1 teaches this fundamental principle of God's love: It includes His obsession with His own glory. The early verses highlight the glory of God in relation to His love:

[God] chose us in [Christ] before the foundation of the world, that we would be holy and blameless before Him. In love He predestined us to adoption as sons through Jesus Christ to Himself, according to the kind intention of His will, to the praise of the glory of His grace, which He freely bestowed on us in the Beloved. (vv. 4–6)

These verses make clear that God's activity in love always coincides with His will, which verse 6 shows to be "the praise of the glory of His grace." The working out of God's will in love results in His glory. And Paul doesn't stop there because this is important. Again in verses 12–14, Paul concludes with God's work in saving us and sealing us with the Holy Spirit by saying all of it is for "the praise of His glory" (v. 14b).

Therefore, to understand fully the love of God, we must understand God's purpose in the universe, since He is love. That's why we can't begin a study on the love of God simply by jumping to 1 Corinthians 13 or 1 John and describing what love does or what it looks like. We need to back up and understand that God's eternal passion is to accomplish His will in such a way that when all has been said and done, He is glorified.

John 13:31 describes the love relationship of the Godhead this way, "Therefore when he had gone out, Jesus said, 'Now is the Son of Man glorified, and God is glorified in Him.'" God can pursue His own glory because He has perfect glory. God does not pursue His glory to gain something He lacks. God has everything He needs. He pursues His own glory because He could aspire to no greater goal than Himself. He is the apex of everything.

Since God's love precedes creation, the only way God could

express His love was within Himself. Therefore, for God to love, He must seek Himself. And in order for God to seek Himself, He must seek His own will and glory. God finds great delight in achieving His will. He doesn't blush about pursuing His own glory. The Bible talks a lot about the delight God gets out of doing things for His own glory. Therefore, God's love can be defined as His self-determination to reflect and manifest His own will and glory.

Make no mistake. Nothing I've said about how much God loves Himself and delights in His glory is meant to imply that God is selfish with His love, hoarding it for Himself. God forbid! But the only reason God can be for you is that God is for Himself. You see, if God were only for you and not for Himself, there would be limits on what He could do.

But since God is pursuing His own glory, when He brings you under the umbrella of His love, you are in the very best position possible. Why? Because as God unfolds His will to achieve His glory in your life, you get to enjoy the blessings of His grace, power, purpose, and joy because you are participating in His love.

When you get the love of God, you will be loved like you've never been loved before—or ever could be. God loves you with the greatest possible love that exists, which is His love for Himself and His passionate concern for His own glory. "From Him and through Him and to Him are all things" (Rom. 11:36).

In Isaiah 43:7, God Himself speaks of Israel, "whom I have created for My glory." He also says that in bringing them back from captivity, He would do something so marvelous that even the "beasts of the field" would glorify Him for it (v. 20). And He promises to wipe out their sins for His own sake (v. 25). This same God loves Israel "with an everlasting love" (Jer. 31:3).

You can't miss the connection between God's love and His glory. God does what He does for His glory. And He's been at it for all eternity. When God created the world, He simply went public with His glory. When God created, He said, "Let me create things outside of Myself that can bring Me the glory I possess within Myself." This allows God to enjoy His own self-love even more, with the result that He can love us as an expression of His glory.

So God spun the universe into existence. In an act of love, He created the world because the most loving thing He could do was to create something that could reflect His glory. God loves us so much that He has given us the privilege of basking in His glory.

When we talk about the love of God, we are talking about the joyful overflow or expression of His will and glory. In His very being, God is perfect love. In His great prayer in John 17, Jesus spoke of the love His Father had for Him before the world began (v. 24). A love relationship exists between the members of the Trinity.

Since God's love is the overflow of His will and glory, whenever His will is done or His glory expressed, God is joyful about it. Jesus said heaven experiences great joy when a sinner repents (see Luke 15:10). Heaven itself is a place of perfect joy. To put it in common terms, God is excited about His glory. You won't fully understand His love until you see that.

GOD'S FULLEST EXPRESSION OF LOVE

God's love finds its fullest manifestation in Christ's provision for the salvation of sinful men. The apostle Paul says this in Romans 5:

> Therefore, having been justified by faith, we have peace with God through our Lord Jesus Christ, through whom also we have obtained our introduction by faith into this grace in which we stand; and we exult in hope of the glory of God. And not only this, but we also exult in our tribulations, knowing that tribulation brings about perseverance; and perseverance, proven character; and proven character, hope; and hope does not disappoint, because the love of God has been poured out within our hearts through the Holy Spirit who was given to us. . . . But God demonstrates His own love toward us, in that while were yet sinners, Christ died for us. (vv. 1–5, 8)

Paul is basically saying, "If you want a visible definition of love, look at what God did for us in Christ." If you really want to understand love, don't watch reality dating shows. Don't listen to people who throw around the term *love* casually. If you want to get to the depths of what it means to love and be loved, look to the death of Christ, because there God's love came to mankind most fully.

Love is to be the hallmark of every kingdom disciple. Jesus not only offered the example for us of what love looks like and to what lengths love will go, but also issued a command to us to follow His lead. In fact, He said that love itself is to be the identifying factor of His followers. This is what He said in John 13:35, "By this all men will know that you are My disciples, if you have love for one another."

Tremendous debate and division has occurred among Christians recently over an historical identification known as *evangelicalism*. Seminary presidents, Bible scholars, thought leaders, and key Christian influencers have spent countless hours and conferences discussing whether the term *evangelical* should be laid to rest. As Fuller Theological Seminary president Mark Labberton said in a speech given at a private meeting of evangelical leaders to address the issue surrounding evangelicalism in our culture today, "We may debate whether the word 'evangelical' can or should be redeemed. But what we must deal with is the current bankruptcy many associate with evangelical life."[3] The so-called "bankruptcy" in the lives of believers can have occurred only due to a lack of alignment with the preeminent identifying factor of our calling: love.

In fact, if a truly biblical term for a Christian group of people were to be sought as evangelicals struggle to decide whether or to keep the name or lose it, the term *agapeticalism* would be far more appropriate. We have been created by a God of love for the purposes of Him expressing His love in order that we might respond in love through loving Him and loving others. That is why we are here. 1 John 4:7–12 describes it this way:

> Beloved, let us love one another, for love is from God;
> and everyone who loves is born of God and knows

---

3. Mark Labberton, "Political Dealing: The Crisis of Evangelicalism," Fuller Theological Seminary (website), April 20, 2018, (original speech given at a private meeting, Wheaton College, Wheaton, IL, April 16, 2018), https:// www.fuller.edu/posts/political-dealing-the-crisis-of-evangelicalism/.

God. The one who does not love does not know God, for God is love. By this the love of God was manifested in us, that God has sent His only begotten Son into the world so that we might live through Him. In this is love, not that we loved God, but that He loved us and sent His Son to be the propitiation for our sins. Beloved, if God so loved us, we also ought to love one another.

God is love. Love is His nature. If we are to reflect God in any way, we must first and foremost reflect His love. And yet far too often, we divide and fiercely debate terminology at the highest levels of our spiritual leadership in our land, and then wonder why our churches lack any real depth or ability to impact our culture for good. John would bring a quick end to many of our ongoing deliberations simply by referring us to the rest of the chapter he penned on this all-inclusive doctrine:

No one has seen God at any time; if we love one another, God abides in us, and His love is perfected in us. By this we know that we abide in Him and He in us, because He has given us of His Spirit. We have seen and testify that the Father has sent the Son to be the Savior of the world.

Whoever confesses that Jesus is the Son of God, God abides in him, and he in God. We have come to know and have believed the love which God has for us. God is love, and the one who abides in love abides in God, and God abides in him. By this, love is perfected with us, so that we may have confidence in the day of judgment; because as He is, so also are we in this world. There is no fear in love; but perfect love casts out fear, because fear involves punishment, and the one who fears is not perfected in love. We love, because He first loved us. If someone says, "I love God," and hates his brother, he is a liar; for the one who does not love his brother whom he has seen, cannot love God whom he has not seen. And this commandment we have from Him, that the one who loves God should love his brother also. (vv. 12–21)

Let me summarize a consequence of this reality: God will determine how much He lovingly involves Himself with you by how much you lovingly involve yourself with others. You cannot have an intimate experience of this attribute of God if you are unwilling to extend His love to anyone else, because God is love. His disciples are to embody and reflect His love. Thus, if you do not know how to love or even if you refuse to love, you will cut yourself off from the full experience of God's love. He restricts the experience of Himself to those believers who are not functioning in love as a lifestyle.

God hangs out with love. So if that is not how you roll, He will not hang out with you. Which is why much of Satan's strategy in the body of Christ is to pull us away from love. Satan encourages selfishness, pride, bitterness, blame, judgment, territorialism, racism, classism, genderism, and envy. Love does not exist in the midst of any of those things. It cannot. Because love is the decision to compassionately, responsibly, and righteously pursue the well-being of another. If your life, thoughts, words, and actions are about only you, then you are not loving as God would have you love. If the Christian life is about only being blessed rather than being a blessing, then you are distancing yourself from God.

One of the reasons so many Christians and so many of our churches are not experiencing God's power is because they are loveless saints. They do not ask the question: How can I love today? To whom can I show love today? And, yes, I understand that you cannot express love to everybody at all times, but you certainly can love somebody anytime. To love is a decision. It is not merely a feeling. It is a decision. That is why I used the term *agapeticalism* rather than *phileoism* or *eroticism* to describe how the Christian church should be identified. *Agape* is a Greco-Christian term referring to the highest level of benevolent and charitable love. It involves actions that benefit others.

First John 3:18 puts it this way: "Little children, let us not love with word or with tongue, but in deed and truth." As Bob Goff puts it, "love does."[4] It's not a feeling.

Yet, when love does not, when you choose not to love, you are hurting not only those who would have benefited from your love, but also yourself. John explains this further in 1 John 3, where he tells us that love opens the door to our prayers and requests of God. He says,

> And whatever we ask we receive from Him, because we keep His commandments and do the things that are pleasing in His sight.
>
> This is His commandment, that we believe in the name of His Son Jesus Christ, and love one another, just as He commanded us. (vv. 22–23)

Guess what? The way to your prayers being answered is to start loving. When Job prayed for his friends, God gave him

4. Bob Goff, *Love Does: Discover a Secretly Incredible Life in an Ordinary World* (Nashville, TN: Thomas Nelson, 2012).

back many of the things he had lost. Job 42:10 says, "After Job had prayed for his friends, the LORD restored his fortunes and gave him twice as much as he had before" (NIV). We all are in this together. And we are here to help each other. Job's friends had caused him great grief and sorrow. Yet God waited until after Job was willing to love them through his prayer on their behalf before restoring what Job wanted back.

Friend, you can go to church until you are blue in the face, but if God doesn't see you loving others, you can forget about your prayer requests. You can sing songs until you are blue in the face, but if God doesn't see love, He may not be listening to much else. God is love. In order to plug in to who He is, you need to live in a lifestyle of love, too.

With the cross of Christ as the ultimate definition of God's love, I want to suggest five elements of *agape* love. If you want to know whether you love God, this will tell you. If you want to know whether you love your mate or anyone else, this will tell you. What God did for us in Christ is the starting and ending point of any definition of love.

Love must have these five criteria to be genuine.

First, agape *love is always visibly expressed.* Love does not just say, "I love you." God expressed His love in creation. You can look around you and see proof of God's love. But as we just discussed, creation isn't the greatest demonstration of His love. God showed His love most clearly in redemption, in Jesus Christ hanging on the cross for all to see. That's the message of Romans 5:8.

Invisible love is no love at all. If people have to read your mind to know you love them, they will never really know they have been loved. True love always can be pointed to. Its activity constantly says, "I love you." So the question is, how are you demonstrating your love? God so loved that He gave us His Son (John 3:16). No demonstration of your love can ever be too costly compared to that!

Second, agape *love is always willing to pay a price for the benefit of another.* John 3:16 reminds us how deeply sacrificial God's love is. If you want to measure your love for someone, or his or her love for you, look at the price tag each person is willing to pay for love. If a man will not sacrifice anything for the woman he claims to love and wishes to marry, he is not the one. If he does not want to be inconvenienced, he is not the one. True love is sacrificial.

A tremendous price tag is attached to true love. Just look at the price Jesus Christ paid. Too many people, though, do not understand or appreciate the price of Calvary. That is why God doesn't get much love back from us. Some people even dare to question whether God loves them. But He says, "Look at the price I paid for you. Look at the fact that when you were hopeless, when you were sinful, when salvation was totally out of your reach, I gave My Son for you. That's how much I love you."

It is safe to say no one else has ever loved you like that. Probably no one else has ever stepped forward to put his or her life on the line so that you might live. No one else has volunteered to take all the strokes of your punishment—especially someone you had mistreated or hurt. We are not into suffering that much.

That's why Jesus Christ so uniquely demonstrates God's love. Christ's sacrifice is crucial to our understanding of God's love, yet we take it for granted. It is good to remember that al-though Jesus' sacrifice for us culminated in His death on the cross, a lot preceded Calvary.

The perfect, spotless Lamb of God lived some thirty-three years in a sinful environment. Try to imagine having to live thirty-three years in a house that has never been cleaned. The house has horrible filth on the carpets, a stench in every room—and you're stuck there for thirty-three years!

God loved us so much that His perfect, sinless Son was willing to live in the stench of a sin-contaminated creation to bring about our salvation. You have to realize how holy God is to appreciate that for Jesus Christ, earth was a stench-filled environment due to sin. In the midst of the contamination, He lived a perfect, sinless life. But then sinful men laid their smelly hands on Christ and took Him away.

They falsely accused Jesus, and then they scourged Him with a horrible, short-handled whip that today we would call a "cat-o'-nine-tails." Threaded into the tails of this Roman scourge were jagged pieces of metal and sharpened bone. The scourging Jesus endured for you and me was not just a whipping that left welts on His back. With every lash, those pieces of metal and bone would dig in and lift out chunks of flesh when the whip was pulled back.

That is why Jesus fell trying to carry the cross to Calvary. He was weak from the beatings and the scourging, and the rubbing of that old rugged cross against the deep wounds in His back made it impossible for Him to carry the weight. The only reason He did so was that you and I were on His mind. He could have called ten thousand angels to His defense.

When He got to Calvary, Jesus was nailed to the cross with spikes through His wrists, not His hands as we so often hear. A spike through the palm would not bear the weight of the body because the hand would tear away.

Jesus' feet were placed on top of one another, and a third spike was driven through one arch, then the other arch, and into the wood. The lifting up of the cross and dropping it with a thud into the hole dug for it must have caused Jesus unbelievable pain. How painful was it? The psalmist said by way of prophecy that all of Christ's bones were out of joint (Ps. 22:14). But He stayed pinned to that cross because you and I were on His mind.

Then Jesus was offered wine mixed with gall, a narcotic mixture designed to dull the senses and make the excruciating pain of crucifixion a little more bearable (see Matt. 27:34). But what did Jesus say? "No. Don't drug Me. I will take the full pain of the punishment. To set sinners free, I have to take their full hell. Don't dull My pain."

Loving God's way involves sacrifice. It costs you something to love. True love is never free. When it comes to love, you must always count the cost.

Third, **agape** *love always seeks to benefit the one loved.* It does not ask first, "What am I going to get out of this?" but "What am I going to put into this so that the one I love can get something out of it?" Godly love "does not seek its own" (1 Cor. 13:5) but rather that which is beneficial to another.

Of course, being sinful creatures we think selfishly and want to know, "What's in it for me?" The fact is there is something for us in true love. Love does not cancel out your own interests, but your benefit is not the focus. Instead, you want to make sure you accomplish a beneficial goal for someone else.

Romans 5:9 reveals a tremendous benefit that Christ purchased for us when He demonstrated God's love. He died for us to save us from "the wrath of God." He had our interests in mind.

God's love is not tied to the worth of the person being loved. If that were the case, none of us would have been saved because Romans 5:8 tells us what our "worth" was before God: "We were yet sinners."

Jesus did not wait until we got better to die for us. He died when we were in our most unlovely state. The person who does not deserve love actually needs love more, not less. If you know someone unworthy of love, you have a chance to emulate Christ because the essence of His love is unconditional.

Fourth, if your love truly reflects God's love, it is not predicated on the other person's earning it, but on your decision to give it. In Deuteronomy 7:7–8, God tells Israel, "[I] did not set [My] love on you nor choose you because you were more in number than any of the peoples . . . but because [I] loved you and kept the oath which [I] swore to your forefathers." God decided to love Israel in a special way in order to advance His kingdom agenda in history. True love does not have to be earned. If it did, God would have stopped loving us a long time ago.

The fact that God's love is unconditional doesn't make it weak and accepting of everything. Here we find a major difference between divine love and what so often passes for love among people. A line from the famous seventies movie *Love Story* goes like this: "Love means never having to say you're sorry."[5] That's poor love and even worse theology.

God's love always makes judgment calls. Paul put it this way: Love "does not rejoice in unrighteousness, but rejoices with the truth" (1 Cor. 13:6). Love hates what is wrong and embraces what is right.

Some people believe that if you love them, you have to accept anything they want to do. No, love always makes judgment calls based on a righteous standard. God is very concerned about right and wrong. That is why in Hebrews 12:6 the writer says, "Whom the Lord loveth, He disciplines" (my translation). Love does not tolerate wrong, so the loving thing to do is to correct. You do not love when you do not correct.

In fact, God says, "If I don't correct you, it's because you are not My child" (see Heb. 12:6). So if you go year after year rebelling against God and never get disciplined, your problem isn't that God hasn't gotten to you yet. Your problem is you are not saved. If you are the devil's child, God may not mess with you. But He says, "If you are My child, I'm going to discipline you because I love you."

Fifth, **agape** *love comes with compassion and emotion.* Don't let anyone tell you that love does not feel. True love always feels. Emotion by itself doesn't equal love, but you cannot have true love without feeling. God feels His love. The Bible says He delights in the works of His hands. He takes great joy in His love for us. Paul says that love "rejoices" when the truth wins out (1 Cor. 13:6). Sometimes we emphasize the caring aspect of *agape* love so much we negate the emotion of it.

5. *Love Story,* directed by Arthur Hiller and John Korty (Paramount Pictures, 1970).

In fact, Paul told the Philippians that he longed for them with "the affection of Christ Jesus" (1:8). Any definition of love that does not include joy and deep feeling is incomplete. It doesn't mean you feel good all the time, but it means that your love is marked by an overriding principle of joy—or even sadness, when it is rejected.

The Bible says that "for the joy set before Him [Jesus] endured the cross" (Heb. 12:2). True love always feels. But please note this crucial distinction: feeling doesn't necessarily mean you love; but if you truly love, you will feel.

Thus, God's love is always visible, sacrificial, beneficial, unconditional, and emotional. So, since God's love is His self-determination to pursue His own will and glory, then to love God is to passionately pursue obeying His will and bringing Him glory. To express that love to others is to compassionately, righteously, and responsibly seek their well-being. When we link into this concept of love, we are positioned to experience God's glorious love at an ever-increasing level.

We may spend the rest of our lives trying to live up to this attribute and calling, but when we abide in Him and His love, nothing is impossible.

Chapter 7

THE WISDOM OF GOD

M aybe by now in this study of our great God you feel as I do, like a kid playing in the sand at the edge of a mighty ocean. Our subject is so vast, because God is so infinite, that we can only scratch around in the sand. But He gave us a pail and a shovel and invited us to dig in, so let's talk about His infinite wisdom.

The wisdom of God is His unique ability to so interrelate His attributes that He accomplishes His predetermined purpose by the best means possible. This definition contains many aspects, so let's break it down a little.

GOD'S WISDOM FLOWS FROM HIS NATURE

God's ability to use His attributes in perfect wisdom is unique because He is the only one who can do it. His attributes, as we have seen before, are His qualities, His perfections, the out-workings of His perfect character. And we know that He has a predetermined plan and purpose He is bringing about for His glory. His power and perfections guarantee that He will always accomplish His plan by the best means possible.

When we talk about wisdom, we refer to more than just knowledge. Wisdom is more than having information. All of us know people who are well educated but just plain lacking sense when it comes to day-to-day living and decision-making. They have a lot of book sense, but no common sense. So simply accumulating data is not having wisdom. Wisdom has to do with the use of the information we have rather than just its possession.

A good example of this use of wisdom appears in Exodus 31:1–5. Israel was building the tabernacle, and one of the skilled artisans doing the work was a man named Bezalel. The Lord told Moses that He had filled Bezalel with "the Spirit of God in wisdom" for all kinds of craftsmanship. In other words, Bezalel knew how to use his skills in the best way possible to make the most of his work and help achieve God's plan for the tabernacle.

When we talk about wisdom, we must consider a specific goal, the best means to reach that goal, and the materials necessary to get there. All three components are embodied in the idea of wisdom. Wisdom is the ability to work with information in such a way that you accomplish the right purpose with that data in the right way.

God's wisdom does not operate outside of His purpose. Paul makes this clear in Ephesians 1:7–11:

> In Him we have redemption through His blood, the forgiveness of our trespasses, according to the riches of His

grace, which He lavished on us. In all wisdom and insight He made known to us the mystery of His will, according to His kind intention which He purposed in Him with a view to an administration suitable to the fullness of the times, that is, the summing up of all things in Christ, things in the heavens and things on the earth. In Him also we have obtained an inheritance, having been predestined according to His purpose who works all things after the counsel of His will.

God's wisdom is tied to His purpose. And Paul states His eternal purpose to be "the summing up of all things in Christ" for His glory. Everything God does in wisdom propels creation toward that one purpose, which is the same in history as it is throughout eternity: His own glory. Since no one is greater than God, and since He has set His own glory as His highest goal, it should not surprise us that He has designed everything to achieve that goal. No one expressed it any better than Paul in Romans 11:33–36:

> Oh, the depth of the riches both of the wisdom and knowledge of God! How unsearchable are His judgments and unfathomable His ways! For who has known the mind of the LORD, or who became His counselor? Or who has first given to Him that it might be paid back to Him again? For from Him and through Him and to Him are all things. To Him be the glory forever. Amen.

Everything that God constructs, He constructs with that goal in mind. Now remember the ingredients of wisdom. Wisdom is arranging things so they meet a goal in the best way possible. God's wisdom so constructs circumstances and people that they all wind up achieving His goal because there is no higher goal to which they could ever go. God is unique in this.

No wonder He is called "the only wise God" (Rom. 16:27). No one else could take all the events of history and so arrange them that they achieve one solitary, all-encompassing purpose. Throughout history, various demagogues, dictators, and power-seekers have tried to bend history to their will and purpose. But they always fail for at least three reasons. First, they are not God, even though some of them think they are. Second, because they are not God, they are not smart enough to pull off their twisted and grandiose plans for very long. And third, they all die some-day. God alone is all-wise.

Friend, you do not have to embrace God's goal. You do not even have to like it—but God will reach it anyway. You could only stop God from reaching His goal by being greater than He is, by having more attributes than He has. Since most of us know better than to try to checkmate God, we would be much better off to cooperate with Him in achieving the goal His wisdom has set. When you do this, life begins to come into alignment.

God moves all events, all people, and all circumstances toward the expansion of His glory. Whether you resist it or cooperate with it, He is still going to achieve His purpose.

Did you know that God will ultimately achieve His purpose even in hell? The people in hell will help achieve the purpose of God, for they will glorify God throughout all eternity. As I said earlier, there are no atheists in hell. Even in hell He will always achieve His purpose of bringing glory to Himself through the manifestation of His wrath.

We touched on this at the opening of a previous chapter. God has an awesome array of attributes. We have studied a few of them, and we have a few to go. God's wisdom is His unique ability to use those attributes in perfect harmony and balance: to blend them together, to take two attributes out over here and add two more over there, to so correlate them that they achieve exactly what He desires.

Daniel 2 shows us this interworking in an interesting way. Daniel has just been given the interpretation of the king's dream, and he praises God for it. Notice that Daniel uses the term "wisdom" coupled with another of God's attributes to show how they operate together: "Then the mystery was revealed to Daniel in a night vision. Then Daniel blessed the God of heaven; Daniel said, 'Let the name of God be blessed forever and ever, for wisdom and power belong to Him'" (vv. 19–20).

God's infinite wisdom worked in tandem with His unlimited power to reveal this secret to Daniel and achieve God's purpose in that situation. But Daniel continues his portrait of our all-wise God:

"It is He who changes the times and the epochs;
He removes kings and establishes kings;
He gives wisdom to wise men,
And knowledge to men of understanding.
"It is He who reveals the profound and hidden things;
He knows what is in the darkness,
And the light dwells with Him.

"To You, O God of my fathers, I give thanks and praise,
For You have given me wisdom and power;
Even now You hast made known to me what we
   requested of You,
For You have made known to us the king's matter."
(vv. 21–23)

In His wisdom, God rearranges people, nations, and situations. Daniel also relates God's wisdom to His omniscience. Because God knows all things, He knows the best choices to make in the outworking of His plan. It takes infinite wisdom to pull that off. More than that, it takes infinite wisdom guiding perfect attributes. I'm not up to that, and neither are you. Only God can do it.

Acts 15:18 puts it this way: "Known unto God are all his works from the beginning of the world" (KJV). Knowing everything in advance puts one in a privileged position. God cannot lose because He knows how the smallest detail will or will not work. He has the whole equation in front of Him, and He can arrange even the smallest details to make everything work.

I am glad we have a wise God putting it all together instead of leaving it up to us because most people don't know or don't care about all the details. When we see a machine with a lot of little parts in it, most of us are not concerned with the parts but simply with whether the machine works.

Your watch is a perfect example. When you want to know the time, you do not open your watch and examine all of its intricacies. You just look at it. But that watch only tells you the right time because intricate parts move together to make the watch work. When was the last time you asked someone to explain to you how a watch works? You only care about the goal: the time.

But the watchmaker is very concerned about the details. He knows that unless the details work together right, the goal will not be achieved. Any manufacturer pays attention to details. God, the manufacturer of the universe, pulls together the details to guarantee that the watch of history achieves its goal: His glory.

God knows the details of all of His works so well that we can have confidence He is going to reach His goal and get there by the best means possible. His wisdom is unique because it allows Him to interrelate His attributes. He can use His characteristics as He needs to do so.

GOD'S WISDOM SEEN IN HISTORY

Let me share with you certain activities in history through which we see the wisdom of God.

For starters, He expresses wisdom through creation. Psalm 104:24 says that "in wisdom" God made all of His works. God's wisdom is clearly seen by creation. In the same way as we can see the wisdom of the watchmaker in the watch, we can see the wisdom of the Earthmaker in the earth. When we see the wonders of this planet, we see a wise God who gave us a home to live in that is perfectly suited to sustain the life that God created. David declares, "The heavens are telling of the glory of God" (Ps. 19:1).

God's wisdom manifests itself in a glorious way in the plan He devised for our salvation in Jesus Christ. In fact, in 1 Corinthians 1, Paul throws some jabs at folks who think they are smart:

For it is written,

> "I will destroy the wisdom of the wise,
> And the cleverness of the clever I will set aside."

> Where is the wise man? Where is the scribe? Where is the debater of this age? Has not God made foolish the wisdom of the world? (vv. 19–20)

None of us would have ever come up with the plan of salvation that God did. In our "wisdom," we would have made it much more confusing, complex, and inequitable. Earn your way to heaven. We would have devised a "layaway" salvation plan. But God designed a salvation free for all, available to all, by sending His Son to die for our sins.

Our wisdom would not have gotten the job done. God had a superior plan, even though the cross looks foolish to a dying world that prefers to depend on its own wisdom:

> For since in the wisdom of God the world through its wisdom did not come to know God, God was well-pleased through the foolishness of the message preached to save those who believe. . . . Because the foolishness of God is wiser than men, and the weakness of God is stronger than men. . . . but God has chosen the foolish things of the world to shame the wise, and God has chosen the weak things of the world to shame the things which are strong, and the base things of the world and the despised God has chosen . . . that no man may boast before God. (vv. 21, 25, 27–29)

In other words, God does not want to share His glory, so He chooses nothingness. He chooses the thing that you would least think of to get the job done. That is why so many things in the Bible do not make sense. You and I wouldn't do it that way. Why does God do it that way? So that He gets the greatest glory. That's why when we believers look among ourselves, we do not see too many of the world's wise and mighty among us.

God did not look just for the rich and the powerful people. In fact, Jesus told us it was easier for a camel to go through the eye of a needle than for a rich man to get to heaven. Why? Because God will never let a rich man flash money in His face at the gates of heaven and expect the gates to fly open. He won't let a power broker flash his power in His face.

Jesus Christ is the wisdom of God in the flesh. The Bible says that in Him "are hidden all the treasures of wisdom and knowledge" (Col. 2:3). In the passage we just considered above, Paul says that Christ "became to us wisdom from God" (1 Cor. 1:30).

GOD'S WISDOM IS MANIFESTED IN THE CHURCH

Here is another way in which God demonstrates His infinite wisdom, through the church:

> To me . . . this grace was given, to preach to the Gentiles the unfathomable riches of Christ, and to bring to light what is the administration of the mystery which for ages has been hidden in God who created all things; so that the manifold wisdom of God might now be made known

through the church to the rulers and the authorities in the heavenly places. This was in accordance with the eternal purpose which He carried out in Christ Jesus our Lord. (Eph. 3:8–11)

Paul says that God's wisdom, which is tied to His purpose, is manifold, the Greek word that means "multicolored," or "variegated," or "many-sided."

As the wisdom of God shines through the church, the church becomes a prism that reveals all the colors and textures of His wisdom. Open the doors of many churches, and you will see a collection of people who, despite all their faults and failures, are the living body of Christ. As a pastor, I can verify that only the wisdom of God could pull that off! God does this to show, through the church, how brilliant and wise He really is.

GOD'S WISDOM IN OUR LIVES

Another way God shows His awesome wisdom is by the way He orders our lives. The Bible uses many illustrations for this. Joseph was sold into slavery and wound up being second in command in Egypt. How did he explain it? Was it luck? A good education? Having a lot of money? No, it was none of these.

Then how did a Jewish slave boy rise to the office of prime minister in Egypt? How did he explain going from the prison house to the White House, from the pit to the palace? Joseph told his brothers, "You meant evil against me, but God meant it for good" (Gen. 50:20).

When God gets in the mix and begins to order your life, He

can even take people who messed you over and use them as a means to accomplish His eternal plan. He is able to take enemies and make them footstools.

I love the book of Esther. The name of God does not appear anywhere in the book, but His thumbprint shows all over it as He ordered Esther's life to achieve His purpose. For example, He made her beautiful so that when King Ahasuerus went looking for a wife, he would choose her.

That way, when Haman plotted to destroy the Jews, Esther would have access to King Ahasuerus's presence as his queen. Her access would then lead to the saving of the Jews and the death of the very man who was out to destroy God's people. Esther's cousin Mordecai got it right when he told her, "Who knows whether you have not attained royalty for such a time as this?" (Est. 4:14). In other words, God ordered all of it. He had a plan to accomplish His glory, including using insomnia to accomplish His kingdom purpose (see Est. 6:1–14).

In 2 Corinthians 1:4–5, Paul says that God gave him his trials so that he could comfort others. In 2 Corinthians 12:7–9, Paul describes his "thorn in the flesh" that God sent in order to humble him. God was going to use Paul so greatly that He had to keep him dependent, so God gave him a thorn he could not get rid of. God ordered Paul's life for a definite purpose.

You may already know James 1 well. But it's so important that I want to look at it again:

> Consider it all joy, my brethren, when you encounter various trials, knowing that the testing of your faith produces endurance. And let endurance have its perfect result, that

you may be perfect and complete, lacking in nothing.

But if any of you lacks wisdom, let him ask of God, who gives to all men generously and without reproach, and it will be given to him. But he must ask in faith without any doubting, for the one who doubts is like the surf of the sea, driven and tossed by the wind. (vv. 2–6)

Can you see what James is saying? When God sends you a trial, He sends it for a reason. Therefore, you can "consider it all joy." That does not mean to be happy that you have a problem. It means be happy that your problem has a purpose. James is talking about those trials that God allows in your life, not the mess you get yourself in through sin.

When God brings a trial into your life, His eternal purpose is that through this test you might bring Him glory. But you bring Him glory by passing the test, not by ducking it or just coasting through. Life operates on this principle, too. You do not get a good career until you pass all the tests. You pass the test in first grade, then in fifth grade, and again in seventh grade. You pass the test to get out of high school; then you must pass the test again and again in college.

All those tests, or trials in our context, are designed to produce in you the knowledge and ability necessary to function in your chosen career. Without the tests, there would be no way to verify your knowledge—and without the knowledge, you could not perform the task. God wants you to perform the task of bringing glory to His name, but without the test you will never know if you have what it takes spiritually to accomplish the task.

But God knows that this creates a problem for us. How do

we handle the trials He sends? That is why the promise of James 1:5 is so important. God offers us His wisdom, and He offers it generously.

Notice, however, that God does not offer you His wisdom so you can figure out how to beat the system and avoid problems. Wisdom has to do with the response you need to make for His glory in the midst of problems. Many people pray the wrong prayer: "Lord, get me out of this trial!"

That is like going to your teacher during final exams and pleading, "Get me out of this room!"

But the teacher's job is not to dismiss you from the test, but to help you successfully complete the test and move on. And the teacher knows that he or she has to keep you in that room despite your protests, or you are going to be a severely handicapped person further down the road.

That is why James cautions, "Let endurance have its perfect result" (v. 4). God will keep you in His classroom until you finish His test. Now if you have taken tests like the ones I have taken, you sit in the room and try to outwait the teacher. But in this case, that cannot happen. You will not outwait God. God is going to stay until you finish the test and you pass. If you fail, you get to retake the test. So you might as well study the first time so you can finish the test and move on.

Let God finish doing what He's doing because He will give you the wisdom you need to pass the test. When you face business decisions, marital challenges, financial setbacks, or emotional trials, God will give you the wisdom to make the response that will bring Him glory. That is why Ephesians 5:17 says, "do not be foolish, but understand what the will of the Lord is." God will show you how to bring Him the most glory by showing you what His will is for you in your time of testing.

Now let me explain a few things about the wisdom God gives. First, we need it constantly. How do I handle this rebellious child? I do not want to be too strict, yet I do not want to be too lenient, either. How do I relate to that difficult coworker? God does not want me to run off and get another job. Every day we face issues like this, so every day we need to be praying for wisdom. God says, "I will grant you My wisdom for handling trials if you will pray for it and be committed to it."

Second, we need to ask in faith (James 1:6). A double-minded person is by definition uncommitted because he is trying to go in two directions at once. He is not sure if he is going to do what God wants done when God reveals it, and God's not going to waste His revelation on people who want to debate Him about it.

God does not want you to say, "Lord, show me what You want me to do so I can decide if I am going to do it." It's got to be, "Lord, show me what You want me to do because I am determined to do Your will. If You show me, I will do it." Many of us do not get our prayers for wisdom answered because we are double-minded. We have not decided ahead of time that we will do what God asks us to do.

A third thing you need to know about God's wisdom is that He gives it one need or trial at a time. To pray "Lord, give me wisdom for this year" or "Help me to live my life wisely" does not really get you anywhere. If anything is clear in James 1, it is that God offers wisdom related to the specific trial that He has allowed.

Fourth and finally, getting God's wisdom does not guarantee that you will figure out why He allowed the trial. I always come back to Job, who never knew why his world fell in on him. He just knew that God was putting him through a heavy trial.

Yet Job acknowledged the Lord's great wisdom and strength (Job 9:4; 12:13; 28:12–27). He said to God, "I'm going to trust You even if You take my life. I'm not going to be double-minded. I don't know why You are doing this to me, but I want You to show me how to walk through it."

That is what God guarantees us, the wisdom to steer our lives over the twisting and sometimes treacherous roads of life (Prov. 3:5–6). If you have ever driven the famous Highway 1 along the California coast, you know what a treacherous piece of road that is. You ride near the edge of the cliff with no guardrails and it goes what feels like a whole mile straight down.

When my family and I were driving Highway 1, my kids told me, "Get off this thing at the next exit!" They were basically saying, "Dad, we have a fundamental problem with your driving skills on regular highways, so we certainly don't want to be at your mercy on Highway 1."

You know what is interesting about driving on roads like that? When you come to a treacherous curve, you do not get into a discussion of why they built this highway like this, why they put this curve here. You do not ask that. Your only concern is to negotiate the curve properly. Getting God's wisdom does not mean you get all the answers. But it will help you navigate the curve that God has put in your path.

So God may not answer the question, "Why have I been single so long?" But He will give you the wisdom to navigate the road of your singleness for as long as He wants you to travel it. He may not answer, "Lord, why did You give me this person to marry? Why didn't You show me all this stuff up front?" But He will give you wisdom to navigate through the turns in your marriage for His glory.

In other words, God's wisdom reveals what His will is for us while we are going through our trial. That often means that He has to spend a lot of time resisting our will. It is like taking your dog for a walk. If you come to a pole and do not pull the dog over, he will keep going around the pole and get tangled. Then when you pull the dog back, instead of coming straight back he will wrap around and come back on your side.

The dog's intentions are good, but now he has himself all tangled. You want him to go forward and the dog wants to go forward, but he is all wrapped up. So what do you have to do to untangle the dog? You have to resist what seems to him the right way to go, pushing him back in the opposite direction to get him headed the right way.

Many of us respond like this to God. We move out in our own direction, and then we get ourselves wrapped around the pole of life and wonder why we cannot move forward. God has to resist us even though we are trying to go the right way, so we wind up praying, "Lord, I'm trying. How come You're resisting me?"

He is resisting us so He can get us unwrapped from ourselves and we can get on with our walk. We have trials because we tend to walk on the wrong side of the pole. Only God in His wisdom can move us forward so that we can achieve His glory.

For my final point, I want to focus on James 3, another great passage of Scripture that lays down a fundamental truth: you cannot mix human wisdom and divine wisdom. God's wisdom is visibly different from the wisdom of this world. That is, you can see what each kind of wisdom produces. Listen to James: "Who among you is wise and understanding? Let him show by his good behavior his deeds in the gentleness of wisdom" (3:13).

To be wise biblically does not necessarily mean to be educated and be able to crank out a lot of knowledge. That is why if you need spiritual advice, you should not necessarily go to the most educated person you know. You may get only sophisticated-sounding ignorance. The most educated person is not always the wisest person. God's wisdom is walk, not talk. It is the ability and decision to apply spiritual truth to life's realities.

James distinguishes between God's wisdom and the world's wisdom:

> But if you have bitter jealousy and selfish ambition in your heart, do not be arrogant and so lie against the truth. This wisdom is not that which comes down from above, but is earthly, natural, demonic. For where jealousy and selfish ambition exist, there is disorder and every evil thing. (vv. 14–16)

Just as there is heavenly wisdom, there is hellish wisdom. James basically says, "It's the way everyone thinks, but it's straight from hell." Notice how he couples the words "natural" and "demonic." So if it is the normal way unsaved people think, then it is born of hell. You would expect a child of the devil to think like his daddy. That is why you cannot be manipulated by what everyone thinks.

This wisdom has visible results. It produces jealousy and selfish ambition. It promotes itself, pushing others down so it can climb up. It is prideful and deceitful. It produces divisiveness instead of unity. The result of worldly wisdom is "disorder and every evil thing."

Do you know why our homes have disorder? Because too many of our marriages and families operate out of envy and ambition. Instead of everyone upholding the central goal of the home, every family member wants his or her agenda. What else can you have but discord? That is earthly wisdom.

A story tells of an infidel who bequeathed all of his property to the devil. The court did not know what to do with the man's will, so the judge said, "The only way to carry out such a will is to order that this farm be left untouched by human hands throughout its history." So they did that, and in a few years, brush and weeds had grown up. The buildings became dilapidated, and the farm was a scene of disorder and ugliness.

This happens to anyone whose life has been willed over to the devil's way of thinking. The weeds begin to grow, and his life becomes dilapidated. He cannot hold his relationships together. He cannot keep weeds from sprouting in his mind. He cannot hold his passions together. He cannot hold anything together.

But James offers us another kind of wisdom, the "wisdom from above" (v. 17), which he says is first of all "pure." That means it is authentic, transparent, clean, like God's Word. Psalm 19:8 says, "The commandment of the LORD is pure."

God's wisdom is also "peaceable," promoting unity and not strife; "gentle," meaning considerate; "reasonable," willing to take instruction, ready to listen to people who make sense; "full of mercy and good fruits," giving practical help to others; "un-wavering," taking a stand on principles instead of flowing one way today and another way tomorrow; and "without hypocrisy," not wearing a mask. That is what a wise person looks like.

Our wise God wants to order your life, and that includes your trials. You will travel your own Highway 1 in life. God will not take you off the road until He has finished with you, but He will teach you how to negotiate the turns. This is why Paul prays that believers would understand and experience more of God's supernatural wisdom (Eph. 1:5–17).

Psalm 90:10–12 says that you can expect to live seventy years—and if you are really strong, you may make it to eighty. Moses prayed, "teach us to number our days, that we may present to You a heart of wisdom."

And if you've taken a wrong turn in life, go to God and say, "I've been unwise." Then get off at the next exit, cross over the highway, and start back down the other way. You cannot change yesterday, but you can make a better choice today. Our God is all wise, and He wants to lead you in His wisdom.

Chapter 8

THE GOODNESS OF GOD

Most of us grew up singing a little chorus that proclaims, "God is so good."[6] That song actually contains some profound theology, because as we will see in this chapter, the goodness of God is one of the infinite attributes of His character.

In fact, God's goodness can be defined as the collective perfections of His nature and the benevolence of His acts. To put it in the words of Psalm 119:68, "You are good and do good." That says it very simply. God is good by nature and good in what He does.

We live in a time when people question the goodness of God. This is not a new problem, however. It really goes back all the way to the Garden of Eden, when Satan informed Eve that the only reason God did not want her to eat from the tree in the

---

6. Paul Makai, "God Is so Good," trans. Marilyn Foulkes (c. 1970), https://hymnary.org/text/god_is_so_good_god_is_so_good.

middle of the garden was that God was selfish. He was not good (Gen. 3:1–7).

Once Satan got Eve to focus on the one tree she could not eat from rather than the many she could enjoy, she lost sight of God's goodness and plunged herself, her family, and the rest of the world into sin.

Something like this happens in many homes with young children at Christmas. Maybe it happened this way in your home. The kids give you their Christmas lists, and let's say they have listed ten things. You buy nine of them. On Christmas morning, the kids begin to unwrap their presents and show excitement about this and that until they discover that item number ten was not under the tree.

It is amazing how quickly the other nine gifts are forgotten and the discussion centers on why you did not buy toy number ten. Suddenly, the kids question your goodness as a parent over the one gift they did not receive rather than the nine they did.

If we are honest with ourselves, we have to admit that we act like that with our heavenly Father. We spend our time complaining about the few perceived desires we do not have rather than rejoicing in the bountiful benefit of the goodness of God that never fails.

To help remedy our problem, I want to discuss five important truths about the goodness of God.

First, the goodness of God is the standard by which anything called good must be judged. Mark 10 makes this remarkably clear because in this chapter, we are confronted with the foundation of goodness. The rich young ruler had it all: wealth, youth, and power, all the things that most people fight to get. But he knew he had a hole inside of him. Something was missing. So one day, he ran up to Jesus and asked the famous question, "Good Teacher, what shall I do to inherit eternal life?" (v. 17).

Jesus' answer in verse 18 is instructive: "Why do you call Me good? No one is good except God alone." The young man was using the term "good" without realizing the full implications of what he was saying or whom he was talking to. He needed a quick theology lesson, so Jesus challenged him, "How do you know I'm good? By what standard are you using this term? You need to understand that no one is really good except God."

Jesus' point to this young man was simply this: "Either I'm not good, or I'm God." Jesus was bringing the young man in through the back door to realize His deity. Aside from this ruler's particular need, Jesus makes the broader point that anything called "good" must find its source in God.

If it—that is, anything you can name—does not emanate from God, does not agree with His nature, it cannot be good because only that which agrees with who and what God is can be called good. It must line up with His perfections and coincide with His revelation and activity, or else it is not good. It does not matter how good something looks or how good it makes you feel; if it is not from God, it is not good.

Far too often in our culture today, if something makes a person feel good for the moment, they think it must be good. You find this philosophy in many places. You hear people argue, "If God did not want me to have it, it would not be here." Such people mistake the mere existence of something for its moral quality. If it's available to them, it has to be good.

But Jesus says to the rich young ruler and to us, "The only

thing that can be called 'good' is that which has its source in God, for nothing is good but God." He is the standard for what is good, not our feelings or experience.

When we used to take the kids home to my parents' house every year in Baltimore for a family vacation, my mom always cooked a big meal. Inevitably she would cook what I call some unholy vegetable, squash or its cousin okra, something that seems to have no purpose in creation. Anyway, when that vegetable bowl came around, I would just pass it right on. But my mom would always ask, "What do you think you're doing?"

I would reply, "But mom, I'm an adult, and I don't want any squash." To which she would reply, "There's no hotel sign outside that front door. This is my house, and you will eat your squash." Then she would take the bowl and start putting the food on my plate for me, like I was a teenager. And she would always put more squash on my plate than I would have taken if I had just done it myself. Then she would say, "And you'd better eat it all."

After my kids would stop their laughing, my mom would cap it all off with this: "It's good for you."

She was right. Medical science will tell you that squash is good for you. I would rather have German chocolate cake à la mode. I can get excited about that. But it is not good for me. Everything that is good does not necessarily taste good, look good, produce nice feelings, or give you a pleasant emotional experience, although many times good things do. The issue of goodness is its source, not its experience.

James 1:17 declares, "Every good thing given and every perfect gift is from above, coming down from the Father of lights." Anything authentically good has its source in the Father of lights "with whom there is no . . . shifting shadow." God produces only that which is good. So if something is not good, it did not come from God. If it is evil, it did not have its source in God.

While God does allow things for reasons we do not always understand, the Bible makes clear that God does not participate in sin in any way. There is no sin in Him. There was no sin in Jesus Christ. God cannot improve. He is good. He does not have to work on His personality, improve His character, or smooth out flaws. He is impeccably perfect in every detail, because God is good. What is more, He finds great joy in His own goodness. He is so good that He can brag about it and be absolutely correct.

The goodness of God is expressed in and through His various attributes. In other words, you know God is good by simply looking at who He is. Let me show you what I mean. In Exodus 33, Moses asked to see God's glory (v. 18), and in response the Lord says, "I Myself will make all My goodness pass before you" (v. 19). Now compare that with Exodus 34:5–7:

> The LORD descended in the cloud and stood there with him as he called upon the name of the LORD. Then the LORD passed by in front of him and proclaimed, "The LORD, the LORD God, compassionate and gracious, slow to anger, and abounding in lovingkindness and truth; who keeps lovingkindness for thousands, who forgives iniquity, transgression and sin; yet He will by no means leave the guilty unpunished, visiting the iniquity of fathers on the children and on the grandchildren to the third and fourth generations."

God tells Moses, "I will let My goodness pass by before you," and then when it happens God says, in essence, "Look at My character."

God expresses His goodness to us by attaching one of His characteristics to the circumstances of our lives. Because God is good, for example, He is patient. In the Bible, patience means not avenging wrong done to you even though you have the power and the right to do so.

You say, "I've got it bad, so God can't be good." No, if God were not good, you would not have anything at all. Because if God were not good, He would not execute patience toward you. And if God did not execute patience, the moment you even thought about a sin, you would drop dead because God is so holy that He has to punish every sin.

You are able to hold this book, and I was able to write it, only because God is patient with us. He has been waiting for years for some of us to come through on our promises to Him. The only reason we are still hanging around and He is still listening to those promises is that He is patient. We would give up on other people a lot sooner than God does.

God's goodness is seen in His love by which He identified with sinful humanity. He gave Himself for us so He could have a love relationship with us. God is so good, He died for you and me. That is pure goodness, and only God has it.

The goodness of God also shows in the fact that He will apply the appropriate part of His character to your situation. Some people like to point out that God once destroyed the whole world with a flood, and they ask, "How could God do that if He's good?"

But they ignore the rest of the story. For years, God warned the people through Noah, "It's going to rain." Noah builds the ark on dry land, a huge ship almost as big as two football fields. He goes into town every day, preaching the same four-word sermon: "It's going to rain." Over and over, year after year, Noah faithfully delivered God's warning.

But our objector might say, "Wait a minute. I can see people going for 120 years and not believing a preacher. Besides, it had never rained before. How were they supposed to know that Noah was telling the truth and it was going to rain?"

Well, even if I did not believe Noah, when I saw the animals lining up two by two to get on that ark, I should figure something big was getting ready to happen. When Mr. and Mrs. Giraffe and Mr. and Mrs. Anteater start saying by their actions, "It's going to rain," I think I would check out what Noah was saying a little closer. All the signs were present, for 120 years. God is good. People want to look at the negative and say, "God can't be good."

He hung in there 120 years waiting for people to repent, and that is not goodness? Someone else will ask, "Will a good and merciful God really send me to hell?" Answer: absolutely. How can He? Because He has begged, pleaded, convicted, even sent His Son to die for you, and you still ignore Him. You see, the issue is not that God is not good. The issue is that people do not want His goodness because they want to make it on their own, to rely on their own goodness. But that is a bad choice.

GOD'S GOODNESS DEMONSTRATED HIS PROVISION

Consider something interesting in Genesis 1:

> God created man in His own image, in the image of God
> He created him; male and female He created them.
> God blessed them; and God said to them, "Be fruitful
> and multiply, and fill the earth, and subdue it; and rule
> over the fish of the sea and over the birds of the sky and
> over every living thing that moves on the earth." Then
> God said, "Behold, I have given you every plant yielding
> seed that is on the surface of all the earth, and every tree
> which has fruit yielding seed; it shall be food for you; and
> to every beast of the earth and to every bird of the sky
> and to every thing that moves on the earth which has life,
> I have given every green plant for food"; and it was so.
> God saw all that He had made, and behold, it was very
> good. And there was evening and there was morning, the
> sixth day. (vv. 27–31)

In His goodness, God not only created you, but also created everything for you. In other words, God did not create the plants, animals, or fish just to have them around. He created them for the benefit of mankind. The earth was created to give us a home to enjoy. Every day when you get up and see the sun shine and say, "What a beautiful day!" God sits back and says, "How do you think that happened? Today didn't just jump up here by itself. It's a beautiful day because I'm a good God."

You eat that fried chicken and you say, "Mmm, that sure was good."

God says, "Hold it. If you read Genesis 1, you will find that I created the water and the dry land. I separated the dry land from the water. I created every fish in every body of water. I created every animal to roam the land. So whenever you eat chicken, don't just say, 'It was good.' Say, 'God is good.'"

Every time you see a rose, God says, "I don't want you just talking about how pretty those roses are, or you miss the point. The point is I know what I'm doing when I make flowers because I am a good God."

When it rains and you say, "It's a bad day," God says, "Hold it! Hold it!" Why? Because Acts 14:17 says He gives the rain and makes the seasons change to bring satisfaction to the human race. No rain, no vegetation; no vegetation, no vegetables or fruit. So the next time you enjoy a vegetable or a piece of fruit, you ought to pause and have a time of prayer and thanksgiving because our good God causes it to rain.

GOD'S GOODNESS MAY DIFFER

God's goodness is not equal. God is good to all in some ways, but He's good to some in special ways. You may need to think about that for a bit.

Matthew 5:45 gives an example of how God is good to all: "He causes His sun to rise on the evil and the good, and sends rain on the righteous and the unrighteous." You do not have to be a Christian to get God's rain. Rain does not fall on just Christians' yards. It rains on all because God has ordained that certain aspects of His goodness be available to atheists as well as to the most committed Christians.

On the other hand, God has provided Christians with the ability to enjoy His goodness in ways that the world can never appreciate. He has given us His revelation, His Holy Spirit to guide us, and a divine perspective on life that opens our eyes to see and enjoy His goodness.

If you are a Christian, you can participate in and benefit from the goodness of God like no unsaved person can. Romans 8:32 says, "He who did not spare His own Son, but delivered Him over for us all, how will He not also with Him freely give us all things?"

Now I realize that to talk about enjoying things makes some Christians nervous. So I want to get something straight about the enjoyment of God's goodness, and I want to get it straight from God's standpoint. Read the verses below carefully:

> But the Spirit explicitly says that in later times some will fall away from the faith, paying attention to deceitful spirits and doctrines of demons, by means of the hypocrisy of liars seared in their own conscience as with a branding iron, men who forbid marriage and advocate abstaining from foods which God has created to be gratefully shared in by those who believe and know the truth. For everything created by God is good, and nothing is to be rejected if it is received with gratitude; for it is sanctified by means of the word of God and prayer. (1 Tim. 4:1–5)

Did you understand Paul's point? It is a sin not to enjoy the goodness of God! Let me repeat that because it is probably a revolutionary thought to some of God's children. It is a sin *not* to enjoy God's goodness. It is a sin to deny His goodness, as these people were doing.

Where does it say sinners get to have the most fun? Many of us were raised to think that when you become a Christian, you enter into a boring existence while sinners enjoy all the good stuff. That is a doctrine from hell. It is a demonic doctrine that says to be a Christian is to live an empty, boring, purposeless, and dull life of denial. It is false because God says, "Everything that I created is good and meant to be enjoyed by those who know the truth."

Believers should be enjoying nature more than nonbelievers do because we know who the Maker is. We should be enjoying relationships more than anyone else does. We should be enjoying a good meal more than anyone else does. We should be enjoying the flowers more than anyone else does. We should be enjoying creation more than anyone else does because we know the Creator. So do not believe this lie that as a Christian you cannot enjoy things.

The issue is not whether we should enjoy the good things our good God gives us. The issue is how we enjoy them. The unbeliever takes and takes from God and does not stop to say thanks or even think about the Giver (Rom. 1:21). But Christians should acknowledge that all good things come from God by thanking Him for them.

Anything you cannot thank God for is not good. Why? Because anything you cannot thank Him for did not come from Him, no matter how good it makes you feel. You should be able to say, "God, I know this came from You."

Notice in verse 5 of the text above that Paul says the good

things we receive from God must be received "with gratitude." When we do that, these things are "sanctified [set apart] by means of the word of God and prayer."

In other words, once you apply God's Word to something as the standard for determining that it is good, and then pray over it as a way of giving it back to God, you have sanctified it. That means God can now get the glory from it because you have set it apart for Him.

Mealtime grace is a good example. Grace has become so dull for many of us because we hurriedly mutter, "Lord, thank You for this food I'm about to receive. In Jesus' name, amen," and dig in. But wait a minute. That meal comes as a gift from a good God. Our prayer should be a way of sanctifying or setting it apart to His glory.

Does that mean we have to give a theology lesson every night at dinner and pray in pious tones while the gravy gets cold? Of course not. But neither should we just go through our day as though all of this is automatic. Sinners do that. God's heart is hurt by the ingratitude of His people.

One of the fundamental reasons we are not passionate Christians is that we are not grateful Christians. We go around all day as though this stuff ought to be the way it is. Do you know any ungrateful kids? They get used to things being a certain way. Then they start to demand things and act as though you have done them a great disservice if you interrupt their cozy routine. Fortunately, most kids grow out of that stage. Some Christians never do.

Too often, we just say, "It's supposed to be there," about whatever God has given to us. As soon as something goes wrong, though, we run to God with the audacity to say, "How could You let this happen to me?"

But God answers, "How can you live day in and day out as though I do not exist, ignoring My goodness?"

That is why so many Christians are tight when it comes to giving either of their service or financial resources. They give God what is left over. They tip Him a little bit of their time and a little bit of their money. Why? Because they are not grateful. Poor giving reflects ingratitude.

Remember the ungrateful kids we talked about? Any kid who refuses to clean his room or wash the dishes is ungrateful. That is the problem you are dealing with, not just laziness. When a child says, "Mom or Dad, cook for me, clean for me, buy me these shoes and those jeans, make sure I'm up on all the new stuff coming out—but don't ask me to do any dishes," that's ingratitude.

The only cure for that is to get a firm grip on the goodness of God. The psalmists knew where their blessings came from. "How great is Thy goodness, which Thou hast stored up for those who fear Thee" (Ps. 31:19 KJV). "No good thing does He withhold from those who walk uprightly" (Ps. 84:11).

God is good because He has provided time and time again. Yet we keep saying "Give me more" when we haven't even gotten around to thanking Him for what He gives us every day because His mercies are new "every morning" (Lam. 3:22–23). Every day should be Thanksgiving for Christians. What a tragedy that Thanksgiving is just a holiday for most.

Now let me point out something of emphasis on the attribute of God known as goodness. You and I live in a contaminated world, and it rubs off. Most of us shower every day because we get dirty, and what is true in the physical realm is true in the spiritual realm. We all get dirty. The effects of a sinful world rub off on us all. That is what makes heaven so great. Heaven will be heaven because no sin will be there.

But because of sin, we live in a very painful world of cancer, disease, dysfunction, personality conflicts, attitude battles, terrorism, and racial strife—the list goes on. We live in a world where if a sinner decides to pick up a gun, a Christian could be in trouble. Much in our world is not good, but it is not because God is not good. It is because man is not good.

Some people will always try to pin the blame on God for the bad things. No, the blame goes to the people who are doing those bad things. We have to understand that even though God is good, it does not mean bad things do not happen. Creation was completely good when it came from God's hand, but it has been contaminated by sin. Therefore, we live in a world where many bad things happen.

Have you ever had your house all clean and then had people come in and mess it up? It is still a good house, but it looks like a mess because of the guests who have invaded it. God created a good world, but it appears to be a mess because the people He has put here to occupy it have been the worst kind of "guests" possible.

How then can God be good when negative circumstances make up so much a part of life in this world? God's goodness does not show only when He does not allow problems to happen. His goodness appears in the fact that even when they do happen, a good God will transcend those negative things and ultimately work out that which will be for His glory and our benefit.

That is why even if your world starts falling apart, the story is not over because God will steer this and shape that to your ultimate good from His perfect perspective. Our problem is that we really do not know what is good for us until we can see in hindsight what God was up to all along.

Children will eat ice cream all day if we let them. To them, many of the things we do as parents do not seem good. Making your kids turn off their smart device and study does not seem good, but they need an education. If we just let God finish what He started, He can turn the negatives to good.

When my oldest son, Anthony, was very small, he had an asthma attack. We took him to the doctor and laid him on the table. The doctor needed to give him a shot, and the needle he brought out was long and intimidating. Anthony saw the doctor beginning to fill the syringe and did a Superman leap off that table and reached out to me. I tried to tell him, "You're sick, and the doctor needs to do this."

Then he began crying, "Daddy, no, no!"

The doctor looked at me and said, "You are going to have to hold him down."

I tried to talk to Anthony a little while longer, but he did not understand. So I had to hold him down. I will never forget the look on his face, which said, "How can you do this to me? How can you join forces with the enemy? How can you help the doctor hurt me?"

I did it because it was good. Painful, yes—but good. Could Anthony understand it? Absolutely not; he was too young, too inexperienced. Could I understand it? Absolutely. I had been that route before. I had those asthma needles stuck in me when I was growing up. I understood that Anthony's temporary pain was necessary to producing long-term health.

God knows the same is true for us. So even when "tribulation, or distress, or persecution, or famine, or nakedness, or peril, or sword" comes along, God so constructs the trial that when it finishes, good results (Rom. 8:35). And through it we become overwhelming conquerors.

Nothing is more exciting than to see a dying Christian who is an overwhelming conqueror. I do not know when I am going to die, but I sure want to die as a conqueror. I want to go like a friend of mine did who knew he was dying and knew there was no medical hope. He looked up and said, "This is my crowning day. Come quickly, Lord Jesus!"

But those who loved him and were looking on wanted to know, "Why did God let him die?" Or, like my beloved wife, as she was transitioning to glory, said loudly, "They are ready to give me my reward."

Do not let anyone tell you that God's goodness has to mean bad things should not happen. God is good because He takes the bad things that happen to us and brings eternal good out of them.

OUR RESPONSE TO GOD'S GOODNESS

My final point is that the goodness of God should motivate His people to worship Him. Consider Psalm 107:1–2:

Oh give thanks to the LORD, for He is good,

For His lovingkindness is everlasting.

Let the redeemed of the LORD say so.

We talk about everything else, don't we? When the big game plays, people are not afraid to let their voices be heard when their team scores. They burst out with praise. Later, they gather together to celebrate their team's victory.

Then God tells us to talk up His goodness and His redemption, and we say, "He already knows I'm grateful." But God does not just want to read your mind or heart. He wants to hear your lips praise and thank Him. You can worship in silence, but praise has to be expressed.

Perhaps you have heard about the husband whose wife asked him, "Honey, do you love me?"

He said, "When we got married thirty-two years ago, I told you I love you. If I change my mind, I'll let you know."

That is not what the wife wants. She wants to hear his love expressed. She wants him to tell her how beautiful she is, that life would not be worth living without her, that she is like the morning sunshine to him, that just seeing her still puts a smile on his face and a gleam in his eyes. God wants to hear from us as well.

We are to come together and celebrate God's goodness. According to Psalm 107:2–3, the people who were to tell of God's goodness were those He had "redeemed from the hand of the adversary and gathered from the lands, from the east and from the west, from the north and from the south." Come together and tell of My redemption, God says. That is worship.

Someone will always answer, "I don't have to go to church to be a Christian." You sure don't. Going to church does not make you a Christian. But if you are a grateful Christian, you will go to church to celebrate God's goodness with other faithful believers. You will not mind singing to His glory. You will shout it out. Why? Because He has been good to you. How can you not sing His praises?

God wants to be praised. You have probably taught your children to say "thank you." But do you just teach them to say it once a week or once a year? Or do you want them to learn to say "thank you" as a way of life, so that it is the exception when they do not express thanks? Parents often say to their kids when they are young and receive something, "I did not hear you say thank you. What do you say?"

God says to us, far too often and even when we are no longer young, "What do you say? I cannot hear you. I do not hear the thanksgiving."

One day, a Puritan was sitting down to a meal of bread and water. Most of us would say, "God, I have only bread and water."

But this Puritan looked down at his plate and said, "Bread and water and Jesus Christ, too! What more can a man ask for?"

Praise is not complete until it has been expressed. The goodness of God gives us ample opportunities to be thankful.

Chapter 9

THE GRACE OF GOD

What would you think if you went to buy a car and the salesman told you that you either had to push the car everywhere you went or pay extra for an engine? You would know something was wrong because cars come equipped with their own supply of power to get you where you are going. The engine is part of the purchase price of the car.

You do have a responsibility to turn on the ignition and steer, but your effort does not supply the power for the trip. When I see so many Christians failing in their Christian life, living defeated lives day after day, month after month, and year after year, it soon becomes apparent they "push" their Christian lives. They do not realize that the power for the Christian life is already under the hood.

That power is the grace of God, His inexhaustible supply of goodness by which He does for us what we could never do for ourselves. Some of us live under the misconception that we have the power to pull off the Christian life. If that were true, we would be no different than a non-Christian who vigorously seeks to keep the Ten Commandments. It is all human effort.

But God has supplied every true believer with a magnificent provision: His inexhaustible supply of goodness called grace. We cannot earn it, we do not deserve it, and you can never repay it, but He has made it abundantly available for free. If Christians need to grasp any truth, it is grace. Grace is not well understood today because the word has been used so flippantly or without a proper understanding of what it involves.

WHY WE MISUNDERSTAND GRACE

One reason most people have problems understanding grace is that they have a misconception about God. Because people do not see God as a holy God, they don't see where they need His grace. They expect to wake up tomorrow morning the way they did this morning, because that is just part of the deal. But many people were here yesterday and aren't today.

Grace means God does not have to do anything. We have seen that He is totally self-sufficient and in need of nothing. Grace means that all you are and all you have comes because He chooses to give it, not because you can demand it or deserve it. Anything we get from God, we get because of His grace. We have to understand that. God owes us nothing. Yet in grace, He has given us an inexhaustible supply of His goodness.

Grace, then, is all that God does for us, independently of us. Grace is absolutely free and cannot be earned (Rev. 21:6; 22:17). People are saved only when they trust in Christ alone, apart from works, for the forgiveness of sin and the gift of eternal life (Eph. 2:8–9; Rom. 4:4–5).

As believers, we have been instructed to grow in grace. Second Peter 3:18 puts it this way: "But grow in the grace and knowledge of our Lord and Savior Jesus Christ. To him be glory both now and forever! Amen" (NIV). To grow in grace means to grow in our experience, understanding, and utilization of grace. Grace is not only a theological term to study. Rather, it is an atmospheric environment in which to live. Sort of like adjusting the thermostat in a room, when you come to know and adopt the mindset of grace, it will change your entire experience of life itself.

Unfortunately, far too many people do not functionally understand this term *grace*. Which is also why so many fail to benefit from it. True, grace is critical in a person's ability to get to heaven, but it is also critical in getting heaven's power and experience down to earth in our everyday lives as we access God's grace through learning to obediently live by faith (Rom. 1:17; 5:2; Heb. 11:6).

When I get on a plane, I watch people all around me pull out their computers to do their work. All the while, I pull out my yellow pad. Whether I am studying, writing, or just taking notes, I use my yellow pad, even though almost everyone else is using a computer. I understand that we live in an age of technology in which we have graduated from yellow pads to computers, but I am stuck in the old covenant of pencils, pens, and yellow pieces of paper. Thus, when I mess up a word, I have to scratch it out and rewrite it. Other people next to me just push a button that cancels out the mistake. When I mess up an entire paragraph,

I have to rewrite the entire paragraph. Others make their old paragraph disappear in a matter of seconds.

What do computers and yellow pads have to do with grace? The reason so many Christians are not experiencing what God wants us to experience is that they are stuck in the old system of the old covenant found in the Old Testament. This system is known as the Law. Yet God is no longer operating in that system. In the New Testament era, under the New Covenant, He ushered in a new dispensation of grace. But when a person refuses to transfer from the old to the new, they willingly relinquish the benefits, blessings, and the power of the Holy Spirit that is tied to the new.

Grace gives victory. It provides the mechanism for peace. It is the producer of joy, the portal of power, the offering of authentic love, the removal of shame, and so much more. Yet unless you choose to grow in, accept, and function in grace, you cannot tap into all of the benefits grace has to offer. Understanding this particular attribute of God and how it carries over into our everyday lives provides you with what you need to fully live out the victorious Christian life.

If your Christian life is miserable, even though you want to be a good Christian, you need to understand grace because it is God's liberating attribute. As you grow in His grace, it will continue to expand in your life, thus giving you more experience of God's reality operating within you.

To understand grace is like a person moving to a new country where freedom flourishes. They have to learn a new language and become used to the freedoms offered to them. Similarly, you and I have to get used to grace because grace is not how

The Grace of God

the world works. Grace is not how we function in our everyday lives. We function through work, earning, and effort. Grace is a different mindset altogether. It operates out of a different frame of reference.

The Greek word *charizomai* means to show favor. That means a synonym for "grace" is "favor." In Greek culture, *charizomai* referred to a superior showing an inferior favor, like a king showing favor to a peasant. A more direct definition of grace is unmerited favor. You cannot earn it. It is the inexhaustible supply of God's goodness whereby He does for us what we could never do for ourselves.

Grace does what rule-keeping under the law could never do. It sets you free. Grace is stronger than your addiction. It is stronger than your sin. It is stronger than your rebellion. It is stronger than that which seems to be holding you hostage. Grace trumps all that because grace gives you and me the ability to tap into the power of what Jesus Christ secured for us on the cross: victory.

The grace of God is possible because of the sacrifice His Son made for the salvation of sinful humanity. We are alive today and not consumed only because of what Jesus did. And we will go to heaven only because of what Jesus did.

If it were not for the sacrifice of Jesus Christ, we would have been wiped out in judgment. But Christ's death on the cross freed God up to shower us with His grace rather than pour on us His holy and justly deserved wrath. We have more of God's goodness than we will ever be able to experience down here.

In fact, the essence of heaven is the uninterrupted enjoyment of God's goodness (Eph. 2:7). We will have glorified bodies that will not get tired because God does not want one second to go by without us thoroughly enjoying the goodness of His grace.

But God's goodness is available in heaven and on earth only because of grace. The reason we worship the Lord Jesus Christ is that because of Him, God's grace was unleashed. We worship Christ because He dealt with the one thing that kept God from extending His grace to us: our sin.

Look at Romans 5, which contrasts the first Adam with the last Adam (Christ). Paul says, "Just as through one man sin entered into the world, and death through sin, and so death spread to all men, because all sinned" (v. 12). In other words, "In Adam all die" (1 Cor. 15:22). We will die because Adam sinned. We were "in Adam" when he sinned. Adam was our titular head—that is, he was our representative.

Now someone may say, "Wait a minute. I didn't choose Adam to represent me. I want to represent myself in this thing. I'm a pretty good person."

But God says, "If you want to represent yourself, you've got a problem. You've sinned too, just like Adam. You haven't done any better than he did" (see Rom. 3:23).

We often hear people say, "Oh, if Adam hadn't done it." But the fact is, if Adam hadn't sinned, we would have done it anyway.

I like the story of the forester named Sam. Sam chopped down trees every day, and every time the boss came by, he would hear Sam saying, "Oh, Adam! Ohh, Adam! Ohhh, Adam!"

One day, the boss asked, "Why do you moan, 'Oh Adam!' every time you're out here chopping trees?"

Sam replied, "Because if Adam hadn't sinned, I wouldn't have to do this backbreaking work, which is part of the curse."

So the boss said to Sam, "Come with me." He took Sam to his palatial home with a tennis court, swimming pool, maid, and butler. "All this is yours, Sam," he said. "You never have to complain again. I give all of it to you, a perfect environment."

Sam could not believe it. The boss said, "Now you can enjoy everything all the time, only don't do one thing. A little box sits on the dining room table. Don't touch it."

Sam went out and played tennis every day, swam, and had his friends over, but after a while, he got bored. There was only one thing in that house he did not know about: that little box on the dining room table. He walked by, checking out the box, but then he reminded himself, "You can't touch it. Don't touch it."

But every day, Sam walked by and saw that box. One day, he finally gave in. "I've got to find out what is in that box." He went over and opened the box, and out flew a little moth. He tried to catch it, but he could not.

When the boss found out that the box had been tampered with, he sent Sam back out to the forest to chop trees. The next day, the boss heard him groaning, "Oh, Sam! Ohh, Sam! Ohhh, Sam!"

Even if Adam had not messed up, we would have because "all have sinned" (Rom. 3:23). We would have to face the issue of death anyway. Turning back to Romans 5, consider what Paul says about the grace of God in Christ that takes the sting out of death:

> But the free gift is not like the transgression. For if by the transgression of the one the many died, much more did the grace of God and the gift by the grace of the one Man, Jesus Christ, abound to the many. . . . For if by the

transgression of the one, death reigned through the one, much more those who receive the abundance of grace and of the gift of righteousness will reign in life through the One, Jesus Christ.

So then as through one transgression there resulted condemnation to all men, even so through one act of righteousness there resulted justification of life to all men. (vv. 15, 17–18)

Thanks to God's gift of grace in Christ, we as Christians do not have to fear death. The Bible describes the death of a Christian as "sleep" (1 Cor. 15:51). Non-Christians die; Christians sleep. The moment you close your eyes, "to be absent from the body [is] to be at home with the Lord" (2 Cor. 5:8). You will never feel death because less than a second after you die, you will be in the presence of God. Death means immediate transferal into glory.

The work of Jesus Christ also brings general benefits to all people. Original sin means that we all are born into this world with the mark of condemnation on us. But the atonement of Jesus Christ for the sins of all people has addressed the effects of the Adamic curse and satisfied the demands of a holy God, so that God is now free to be good even to sinful people.

Please note, I did not say that all people are automatically saved by Christ's death. Every person will be judged on the basis of how he or she responded to Christ (John 3:18–19). Those who reject Him will face condemnation. I am not talking about salvation benefits, but what is often called "common grace." For instance, Jesus says that God causes the sun to shine and the rain to fall on the unrighteous as well as the righteous (Matt.

5:45). And Jesus' light, without exception, shines on every person in the world, making all people saveable (John 1:9; 1 John 2:2; 1 Tim. 4:10). That is part of God's common grace to all. So is the air. You do not have to be a Christian to get oxygen. God gives common grace to all. But He reserves His special grace for those who trust Christ alone as their personal sin-bearer.

God gives common benefits to the whole human race, but the benefits of His special grace come only to His children. Again, these flow to us through our relationship with Jesus Christ.

Everything good comes from God, and only because Jesus Christ freed Him up to give it by satisfying His just wrath against sin (2 Cor. 5:21; 1 John 2:2). Non-Christians will not always thank God for the air, water, and sunshine that keep them alive, but everyone who names the name of Christ should wake up each morning thanking God for His grace. We know it is all because Jesus Christ satisfied the demands of a holy God. So first of all, grace is possible only because of Christ.

Next, God's mercy is distinct from His grace in that grace means giving a person something he does not deserve, while mercy is identifying with someone's misery and not giving them what they do deserve. According to Ephesians 2:4–5:

> But God, being rich in mercy, because of His great love with which He loved us, even when we were dead in our transgressions, made us alive together with Christ (by grace you have been saved).

Here, Paul beautifully juxtaposes grace and mercy. In mercy, God's heart went out to us in our helpless condition. In grace, He gave us what we did not deserve, and could not earn—salvation.

Every misery we experience in life is, to some degree, related to sin—either our own sin, someone else's sin, or just the contaminated, sinful world in which we live. Because He is "rich in mercy," when God sees our pain, He feels it. He experiences it with us. But grace must precede mercy because God cannot help us with our misery until He first deals with our sin.

Often, someone will come to one of the staff members in the counseling ministry at our church in Dallas and say, "Help me! This problem is making me unhappy, discouraged, depressed, and frustrated. It's making me miserable." We have to tell that person he or she can find no divine relief for misery, no matter who the counselor is, unless the sin question has been addressed.

That is because God's grace must deal with sin before God's mercy can quell the miserable effects of sin. Once God has dealt with us in grace, He can act toward us in mercy. You would not think much of a doctor who was only willing to deal with the symptoms of a serious illness without looking at the source of the disease that caused those symptoms. If you want God's mercy to deal with your misery, you first must accept His grace to deal with your sin.

That is why John wrote to Christians, "If we confess our sins, He is faithful and righteous to forgive us our sins and to cleanse us from all unrighteousness" (1 John 1:9). Confession of your sin frees God to show you His mercy. If you are miserable, you need God's mercy. But you cannot have His mercy until you have allowed His grace to take away your sin. Once you have come clean with God, He is able to help you with the things that bring hurt.

Mercy happens when God not only deals with your need, but goes overboard and deals with the effects of that need in your life. We need that because many of us have made decisions or had experiences that have messed us up. Maybe abuse by a parent, some rebellion on your part, or something that you should not have done has caused you real problems. It could be emotional, mental, or physical problems that have created misery for you. God is free to help you because He is full of mercy, the result of His great grace. The Bible says that God's mercies are "new every morning" (Lam. 3:23).

Every day, God has something new to show you as He deals with some aspect of your life. The problem is we are not looking for it, so we seldom see it. If we would be fully aware of what God does in one twenty-four-hour period, we would be amazed at how many things He does to relieve some of the burden for us. We dismiss so much of what happens to us as ordinary or even chance. But the verse just before the one I quoted above says, "It is of the LORD's mercies that we are not consumed" (Lam. 3:22 KJV).

Every day you wake up, it is by the mercy of God. We all have made promises to God: "Lord, if You'll get me out of this . . . if You'll solve this problem . . . if You'll raise me from this sickbed . . . if You'll give me a good doctor's report . . . I'll serve You the rest of my life."

We fail to keep many of our promises. So why doesn't God take us out? Because of His mercy. And why can God show us mercy? Because of grace. Because He looks at Jesus Christ and is so satisfied with Him, He is able to deal with us in mercy and pity us in our sin and pain. No one wants what he or she deserves. Does a guilty person throw himself on the justice of the court? Of course not. He throws himself on the mercy of the court.

That is what we do when we cry out to God and say, "Lord, I messed up. It was my sin that got me in here, or the sin of someone else, but I plead the blood of Jesus Christ. Have mercy on me!"

The Israelites cried out to God from the misery of Egyptian slavery, and their cry reached not only His ear, but His heart. So He sent Moses to deliver them (Ex. 3:9–10). Those Israelite slaves wanted mercy. So should we.

With lives like ours, we do not need justice; we need mercy. God is free to pity you in your pain, walk with you in your struggle, and hurt where you hurt because His great grace has unleashed His great mercy.

LIVING IN GRACE

You should memorize this verse: "And God is able to make all grace abound to you, so that always having all sufficiency in everything, you may have an abundance for every good deed" (2 Cor. 9:8). God has something for everything you need. There is no such thing as insufficient grace.

Many of us have suffered the embarrassment of bouncing a check because of insufficient funds. But God has no problem covering His checks. The Bible says that God's grace is so inexhaustible, so awesome in its supply, it never runs out. Grace is designed not only to save you, but also to keep you. When you became a Christian, God supplied you everything you needed for spiritual life and growth.

That is why Peter says, as we saw earlier, to "grow in the

grace and knowledge of our Lord and Savior Jesus Christ" (2 Peter 3:18). Peter is saying, "Grow in your understanding and utilization of grace. The more you understand about grace, the more you enjoy the Christian life." Do not let anyone stop you from growing in your understanding of the awesome supply of God's grace.

The story is told of a man who was given a free ticket for an ocean cruise. The fare took all of his money, leaving him nothing for meals on the weeklong trip. So he brought peanut butter and jelly sandwiches with him, and while his fellow passengers enjoyed sumptuous meals and buffets every evening, he went to his cabin in embarrassment and ate his meager meals.

The man was miserable knowing that everyone else was eating this incredible food, but he knew he could not enjoy any of it because he had used all of his money for his ticket. At the end of the cruise, as the man was leaving the ship, one of the porters asked him, "How did you enjoy the cruise?"

He said, "Well, I loved the ride, but I was always hungry because I couldn't afford any of the food."

The porter looked at him in astonishment and replied, "Sir, the meals were included in the price of your ticket! You were miserable for no reason at all."

I think when a lot of us get to heaven, God will say, "You were miserable for no reason at all. All of your answers were available in My all-sufficient grace. But you didn't grow in grace and never came to understand My sufficiency." When you met Jesus Christ, everything you need for your Christian life was included in the free salvation "ticket" He gave you. But if you don't grow in grace, you don't know or experience all the goodness God has supplied for you.

Many "spiritually millionaire" Christians live pauper lives because they have not grown in their understanding of God's great, inexhaustible supply that was provided in Christ. Do not let anyone stop you from maximizing your Christian experience. Would anyone do that? I do not want to shock you, but you need to know that some Christians think their calling is to make you spiritually miserable. They are not going anywhere spiritually, and they want company. But God says, "My grace is sufficient."

Paul learned this truth in the midst of a problem:

> because of the surpassing greatness of the revelations, for this reason, to keep me from exalting myself, there was given me a thorn in the flesh, a messenger of Satan to torment me—to keep me from exalting myself! (2 Cor. 12:7)

We are not quite sure what Paul's thorn was, whether a physical ailment like bad eyes or even a person who was trying to discredit him. Whatever it was, he struggled with it. It was number one on his prayer list for some time. He tells us,

> Concerning this I implored the Lord three times that it might leave me. And He has said to me, "My grace is sufficient for you, for power is perfected in weakness." (vv. 8–9)

I am confident you have a "thorn" somewhere in your life. Maybe your thorn is a person who keeps pricking you, a problem you cannot get over, or an illness the doctors cannot heal. God says His grace does not always remove these things, but it does empower you to overcome them.

God's grace is not a "disappearing cream" you rub on problems. It raises you above the problem and gives you power and enablement at the exact point where most people would quit.

God's grace enables us to love people we would normally hate, to have patience when we would usually give up. Grace gives us power we did not have before. Grace does not only remove problems. Sometimes it helps us plow through them. But it is still grace because we could not have done it without God.

My question to you is, what did you do last week, last month, or last year that only God could have pulled off? If you cannot point to something in your life that only God could have done, you are not growing in grace. You still live in your own power. You push your car rather than letting grace do the work.

The grace of God also trains us in how to live the victorious Christian life. Paul says in Titus 2:11, "For the grace of God has appeared, bringing salvation to all men." The appearance of God's grace Paul talks about is the coming of Jesus Christ to earth to die for us and bring us salvation. Jesus Christ is grace personified; therefore, the more you grow in Him, the greater degree of grace you experience. But look at what else God's grace does for us:

> Instructing us to deny ungodliness and worldly desires and to live sensibly, righteously and godly in the present age, looking for the blessed hope and the appearing of the glory of our great God and Savior, Christ Jesus. (vv. 12–13)

Grace instructs us in how to live. Grace is much more than a concept. It is an environment in which we live and move. In his tearful goodbye to the elders at Miletus, Paul commended them to "the word of [God's] grace, which is able to build you up" (Acts 20:32). He said this in the context of their responsibility to the church, to guard God's flock. These men were going to need real spiritual strength to do their jobs.

That is what grace does. Grace will give you victory where you did not have victory. Grace will give you power where you did not have power. Grace will give you the ability to keep on keeping on when you want to give up. And grace will always lead you to pleasing God (that is, godliness) rather than being an excuse to sin (Rom. 6:1).

Grace teaches us how to live. It gives us not only the right information but also the right enablement. With grace comes power; it has batteries. A lot of people can give out right information. After all, we are on the "information superhighway." The trouble is this highway has no gas stations. Where do we get the power to pull this off?

Grace gives it to you, Paul teaches. He explained it to the Galatians this way:

> I have been crucified with Christ; and it is no longer I who live, but Christ lives in me; and the life which I now live in the flesh I live by faith in the Son of God, who loved me, and gave Himself up for me. (2:20)

In other words, "I have exchanged my life for Christ's life living in me." Notice he goes on to say in verse 21 that this kept him from "nullify[ing] the grace of God."

Living the Christian life in your own power nullifies the operation of grace in your life. If you try to pull yourself up spiritually by your own good works, by positive thinking, or by sheer
determination, you cancel out God's grace.

It is no accident that Paul wrote this way to the believers in
Galatia. In the very next sentence he said, "You foolish Galatians, who has bewitched you, before whose eyes Jesus Christ
was publicly portrayed as crucified?" (3:1). They were being
tricked by people who had exchanged inner spiritual power for
outward religious conformity. If you are making that same exchange today, you have been tricked.

What is the solution? Paul reveals it in Galatians 5:1: "It was
for freedom that Christ set us free; therefore keep standing firm
and do not be subject again to a yoke of slavery."

Here is an expanded Evans translation: "Don't let anyone
enslave you. When you were set free by Christ, you were free to
do what you ought to do. You were set free by Christ to enjoy
Christ's life in you. Don't let anyone put a magical spell on you.
Don't let anyone enslave you to thoughts, actions, or patterns
that are not in agreement with Christ. You are free now. Don't
let anyone tie you up." Jesus told His disciples, "Apart from Me
you can do nothing" (John 15:5).

Some Christians are tied up in knots trying to live by other
people's religious rules rather than by grace. Paul tells us to let
grace, not people, govern our lives. Galatians 5:2 shows how
critically important this is. "Behold I, Paul, say to you that if you
receive circumcision, Christ will be of no benefit to you." Verse 4
carries on the startling thought: "You have been severed from

Christ, you who are seeking to be justified by law; you have fallen from grace."

So it is possible for us as Christians to go back to an external rule of conformity, and in so doing cancel out the power of Christ and the free-flow of grace in our lives. Some of us who are trying to do good have cut off the power of Christ because we operate by our external conformity and determination rather than by the inner dynamic of grace. We are driven by law-keeping rather than by relationship. In addition, worldliness can limit or block the flow of grace in our lives (James 4:4–10).

What does it mean to fall from grace? It means you no longer live by the grace standard, but by the flesh standard. You try to do in the flesh (that is, human effort) what can be done only by the power of God. To the degree that you are in deep relationship with Christ, you will have the power to live the victorious Christian life (John 15:1–16).

Do not misunderstand me. Nothing is wrong with legitimate rules. Rules are necessary, but the power to obey them must come from within. The idea is not to get rid of legitimate rules, but to get back into relationship with Christ so that we will have the proper motivation and enablement to do the things that would please the Lord.

Grace never means people hold no responsibility. That's called lawlessness. The difference between living under grace and living under law is that under grace, we are motivated to obey by the proper power source, which is the Spirit. That is the engine underneath the hood. The Bible calls it the filling of the Holy Spirit (Eph. 5:18). By the way, the verb there indicates that filling is to be a continuous process. Life under the law depends upon human effort, not spiritual empowerment.

But it is like filling your car with gas. Your tank may be full now, but if you just keep going and going, you will run low on gas. We just keep living the Christian life without continually being refueled by our relationship with God, and then we wonder why our lives become stalled spiritually.

I can relate to this because I regularly drive on fumes. I can usually tell how far past empty the gas tank needle can go before I need to fill up. One time, though, I guessed wrong and ran out of gas on Interstate 35 in Dallas. I started to chug along and finally had to pull over to the side. I looked down and, sure enough, I was out of gas.

If you do not keep your spiritual tank full, do not be surprised if you end up on the side of the road. We have got to keep fueled up, so to speak, if we want to know the enabling power of God's grace. We ought to be constantly saying, "Boy, I don't know where I got the ability to do that." Just saying it will remind you where you got it—the grace of God.

So as our relationship with Christ is cultivated, we grow in grace. Then the supply of grace, energized by the power of the Holy Spirit, gives us spiritual victory. At that point we can say with Paul, "By the grace of God I am what I am" (1 Cor. 15:10). When grace starts operating, we will begin to sing when it is not Sunday, serve without being asked (1 Peter 4:10–11), and know how to speak to others with a voice of grace (Col. 4:6). We give grace because we have experienced grace.

The grace of God is experienced only by those who receive it on His terms. James 4:1–2 says,

What is the source of quarrels and conflicts among you? Is not the source your pleasures that wage war in your members? You lust and do not have; so you commit murder. You are envious and cannot obtain; so you fight and quarrel. You do not have because you do not ask.

The first way you experience God's grace is by asking for it. But too many of us try to make things happen on our own, fussing, fighting, and forcing to get what we want. How many husbands and wives fight to change one another? Or struggle to make this happen and that happen? "You are warring," James says, "when all you have to do is ask."

It is of course possible to ask "with wrong motives, so that you may spend it on your pleasures" (v. 3). We tend to think of this as asking for material things. We think, "Sure, I can understand God not giving me a sports car." But this can apply to all kinds of prayers we make that are designed not to glorify Him, but only to benefit ourselves.

I keep coming back to children as an illustration because so much of what we do as Christians is similar to what kids do. Kids ask mostly for things for themselves. And when they get them, they are usually not too eager to share.

James basically tells us, "One reason you are defeated and don't have a lot of things necessary for you to be victorious is that you don't ask. And when you do ask, you ask too often only to benefit yourself. You are using human methods. Ask, but with the right motives."

Then he says in verse 4,

You adulteresses, do you not know that friendship with the world is hostility toward God? Therefore whoever wishes to be a friend of the world makes himself an enemy of God.

You cannot love the world and love God at the same time. You have to make a choice. No compromise is possible. You cannot have the world and God too; that it spiritual adultery, James warns. Our God is jealous of His work in us (v. 5). He will not share us with another spiritual suitor—and He should not have to!

Then James makes a statement about grace: "But He gives a greater grace. Therefore it says, 'God is opposed to the proud, but gives grace to the humble'" (v. 6).

If you think you can do it yourself, God says, "Okay, do it yourself. If you can't do it yourself, come to Me." That is humility. Humility recognizes that I have a need I cannot meet by myself. It says, "God, I need You to meet it for me." As long as you think you can do it yourself, you are being prideful. And God opposes the proud.

You do not want God opposing you. He will make it impossible for you to do what you want to do through the methods you are trying to use. He is going to resist you because God will resist His children who operate independently of Him, who do not ask, who compromise with the world. But the humble cry, "I can't. I need You. I'm desperate!" To them He gives more grace.

Hebrews 4:16 says, "Therefore let us draw near with confidence to the throne of grace, so that we may receive mercy and find grace to help in time of need." You can go to a place called the "throne room of grace." It is like a bank. It stores up whatever you need to pay whatever bills you need paid. In this throne room, God dispenses grace, but only upon request.

When was the last time the bank called you and asked, "Do you need some money?"

It is generally you going to the bank saying, "I need some money."

God says, "I've got a throne room called grace. Do you need grace? Then draw near that you may receive mercy and grace in the time of need." How long do you stay there? Until you get what you need. If it is important enough, you will stay.

When chain saws were first available, a man who was used to chopping trees by hand went to a hardware store. The proprietor said, "We have a new power saw. With this saw, you can cut down thirty trees a day instead of the three you're doing now."

The man said, "Are you serious?"

"Yes, thirty trees a day with this power saw."

"I'll take one." He bought the power saw, but came back mad a week later. "Why did you sell me this piece of junk?"

The proprietor asked, "What's wrong?"

"It took me a week to cut down one tree with this piece of junk. I was better off using my old axe!"

The proprietor said, "Let me see it." He took the saw, pulled on the cord, and it started right up with its motor roaring.

The man jumped back and asked, "What's that noise?"

You do not buy a power saw so you can go out and put even more human effort into cutting down trees. You buy a power saw to let the motor empower the cutting. God did not save you so you could continue trying life on your own. Nor did He save you so you could seek to keep that salvation through your own works. That is not possible. The grace of God both saves and keeps you secure through your faith alone in Christ alone. When you live in this truth, God displays His power and His strength in your life as you depend on Him and, through obedience, cooperate with His enabling grace.

What a shame to have God's Spirit but chop down only one need in your life, when enough power has been made available to chop down a hundred needs. This is the provision of God's grace.

Chapter 10

THE GLORY OF GOD

When was the last time you took a breath? How about the last time your body pumped blood throughout your veins? Can you recall the last time sleep restored and refreshed you? Or when was the last time you ate?

You might be shaking your head at the seemingly strange line of questions. Of course you can recall the last time each of those things happened because they happen all the time. The average person takes around 25,000 breaths every single day. The average adult heart pumps around 2,000 gallons of blood each day. Most of us sleep every single night, just like most of us eat every single day.

Yet if God were to remove just one of those provisions from the equation for any of us, life as we know it would be over. One of the greatest problems we face in recognizing and participating in the purpose of this all-important attribute of God—His glory—is that we take God for granted. He is so consistent at what He does that we forget how amazing He truly is.

One reason why God goes underappreciated by many of us is that He is so reliable. He has supplied air every single day for thousands upon thousands of years. The sun has been shining all the time for thousands upon thousands of years. The earth has not spun too fast or too slow to either make us dizzy or throw us off for thousands upon thousands of years. We get rain when we need it so that food can grow. We have animals that provide food, work, or companionship. God is so good at being God that we often forget He is God and, as a result, fail to give Him the glory He deserves.

In fact, if God took a break once, if He just said, "I'm going to sit this day out," it all would be over. Yet because His mercies are new every morning and His provision comes through every moment, His glory goes unnoticed, ignored, and unappreciated.

Before we get much further into this final attribute of God, let me define it. Glory is the process of manifesting, demonstrating one's attributes. In sports, it involves letting everyone in the stands see you strut your stuff. Or for celebrities, it is letting people in on who you are and your best qualities. That is glory in human terms.

But the glory of God is best described as the visible manifestation of His attributes, His character, His perfections. The word translated "glory" in the Old Testament is very interesting. It means "to be weighted, to be heavy." We would probably use the word "awesome" today. God is glorious. He is, to put it quite bluntly, awesome.

His glory is the sum total of His intrinsic nature. When I talk about the glory of God, I mean the comprehensive grouping and expression of all that makes Him who He is, the sum of His being. God's glory is unique because it is intrinsic in nature. Let me put it another way: God's glory is self-defined, self-initiated, and self-expressed. You do not have to "give" God glory for Him to be glorious. Neither does God need to develop His glory as an athlete or scholar would. Every human being who has risen to the point of celebrity or "glory" started from the beginning. Michael Jordan began by practicing dribbling the ball. Tom Brady began by tossing the ball to his dad when he was a kid. Every scientist who ever invented anything began by learning the alphabet. Not so with God. God started off with His intrinsic glory, and He left Himself no room for improvement. But, in all actuality, I cannot even say that God "started off" with glory because God never "started" at all. There is never a time when God has not been because He exists eternally in another dimension. You and I live in time, and so we cannot understand or appreciate that reality yet. But God is so glorious, He never had to nor will have to go outside of Himself to make Himself better at what He is.

Maybe this will help you see it more clearly: What wet is to water and heat is to fire, glory is to God. Water does not have to find wet to be wet. It just is wet. Fire does not have to find heat to be hot; fire is always hot. Wetness and heat are intrinsically interconnected with water and heat. Similarly, glory is intrinsic to God. He never will not be glorious. He is glory.

God is the only being in existence who is not dependent upon something outside of Himself to exist. He generates Himself by Himself within Himself. That is why He says in Isaiah 48:11, "For my own sake, for my own sake, I do this. How can I let myself be defamed? I will not yield my glory to another"

(NIV). No one compares to God, which is why He is insulted when His glory is challenged by humanity. When you or I place anything above God in our hearts, it becomes idolatry rooted in pride. God hates pride. He will not stand for it. That is why the principles in Proverbs 16:18 show up in people's lives time and time again: "Pride goes before destruction, a haughty spirit before a fall" (NIV).

God will not share His glory with another. In fact, we have been created to reflect His glory back to Him. That is why we are here. If anyone you know is ever confused about the meaning of life, it is fairly simple. Our purpose is to glorify God. Isaiah 43:7 is everyone's life verse, whether they know it or not: "Everyone who is called by my name, whom I created for my glory, whom I formed and made" (NIV).

The reason God created us was for His glory.

Pause for a moment and let that sink in because that is the problem that plagues us. The problem is that most people do not define their existence by that which is to bring God glory. But that is why we are here. God created humanity in His image to reflect His glory back to Him. God wanted to look at Himself in a mirror through earth-bound creatures in order that we might bounce back His glory to those around us and to Him.

You were created for God's glory. We all were. Which means that any man, woman, boy, or girl who is not living for the glory of God does not know why they are here. Yet what Satan has sought to do is corrupt our thinking and our souls through introducing a self-centered definition of purpose. Satan knows if he can get our eyes off of God's glory and onto our own, he has won the battle. That is why Paul defines sin as an interruption in the glory of God. Romans 3:23 says, "for all have sinned and fall short of the glory of God." Sin detracts from glory. It causes a gap in our reflection of God's glory. And I am not talking about just big, public sins that are easy to point fingers at. I am talking about all sin, especially those like pride, doubt, envy, lust, and more. Each sin Satan can lure you into committing keeps you from living out your purpose, which is to reflect God as His image-bearer, and by so doing, display His glory. You and I have been created as divine advertisements because glory means to "put on display." Essentially, you and I are God's ad agency. We are to be advertisements of His radiance in all that we say and do.

First Corinthians 10:31 puts it this way: "So whether you eat or drink or whatever you do, do it all for the glory of God" (NIV). Now, eating and drinking are two of the most mundane things we do. But that is why we need this Scripture to remind us why we are here. God put us here to bring Him glory, and we are not even to drink a glass of water independent of our recognition of Him. This makes sense, though, when you consider that if any of us were to stop eating or drinking, we would not be able to do much else after that. All we do is to reflect His glory back to Him because all we do is done because He enables us to do it.

What is more, when we radiate God's glory back to Him, we get to experience His glory at a greater level in our own lives.

SHEKINAH GLORY

The Jews had a word for God's radiance reflected in all of humanity's experience. They called it the *shekinah* glory. The word *shekinah* means "to dwell or reside with," the glory of God residing with humanity so we can see and experience it.

This is a vital point, and I want to do it justice theologically without overstating the case, so stay with me for a moment. If you could pull out the nucleus of God, so to speak, His internal essence would be a huge, radiating light. If God were to come to us and show us His inner self, we would see a big light. Where do I get that? Listen to Paul describing to Timothy God's inner essence as he discusses the second coming of Jesus Christ:

> Which He will bring about at the proper time—He who is the blessed and only Sovereign, the King of kings and Lord of lords, who alone possesses immortality and dwells in unapproachable light, whom no man has seen or can see. To Him be honor and eternal dominion! Amen. (1 Tim. 6:15–16)

God's inner core is a radiating, unapproachable light. This explains why God created the sun with its "unapproachable light" to rule the day. The earth is 93 million miles from the sun, but you could not get within a million miles of the sun without burning to a crisp. The sun is that hot; that much gas comes out of that big ball of fire. That is all the sun is, a big ball of fire with so much power and so much light that it lights the whole world and will burn you to a crisp from a million miles away.

Now you understand what God meant when He said, "no man can see Me and live!" (Ex. 33:20). You would disintegrate because at His core, "God is Light" (1 John 1:5). That is why whenever God shows up in history, it is always in relation to light.

For example, when Ezekiel saw the glory of God, he said it

was like a "surrounding radiance" and the prophet fell on his face (Ez. 1:28). When the shepherds were in the field at the birth of Jesus, "the glory of the Lord shone around them" (Luke 2:9). And concerning the New Jerusalem, the Bible says, "the city has no need of the sun or of the moon to shine on it, for the glory of God has illumined it" (Rev. 21:23).

God reveals the light of His glory in a number of ways. The first of these I want to look at is creation. In Psalm 19, the classic passage on this truth, the psalmist says,

> The heavens are telling of the glory of God;
> And their expanse is declaring the work of His hands.
> Day to day pours forth speech,
> And night to night reveals knowledge. . . .
> Their line has gone out through all the earth,
> And their utterances to the end of the world.
> In them He has placed a tent for the sun,
> Which is as a bridegroom coming out of his chamber;
> It rejoices as a strong man to run his course.
> Its rising is from one end of the heavens,
> And its circuit to the other end of them;
> And there is nothing hidden from its heat. (vv. 1–2, 4–6)

In the same way that nothing is hidden from the sun, nothing can hide from God's glory. God says, "If you want to see how great I am, go outside. The heavens tell of My glory." We get confused because we talk about Mother Nature, not Father God. God says we can see His glory simply by looking at His creation. You only have to go outside, and the heavens will tell you a story about the glory of God.

And what a story they tell! For example, on a clear night, if you could look at the whole sky covering the earth at one time, you could see about three thousand stars with the naked eye. But scientists with their telescopes can see to the edge of the Milky Way, and they have calculated that our galaxy alone houses two hundred billion stars. And those same scientists estimate that the universe contains at least one million other galaxies like the Milky Way.

Now let's go back. With your naked eye, you could see three thousand stars. That means God is pretty sharp. With the telescope, we can "guesstimate" two hundred billion stars in our Milky Way. God's getting bigger and bigger. But if a million other galaxies hang in space, we are talking about a God of glory! This God created the universe to display His glory, and it did not take Him long to do it either. He just said, "Let there be light." That's how glorious our God is.

God's glory can be seen in the vastness of space, and it is also seen in life's particulars. It is seen when snowflakes fall. It is seen in the fact that no two people have the same fingerprints. It is seen in the fact that when the earth spins on its axis, it does not spin too fast, lest we be thrown off course. It does not spin too slowly, lest we become dizzy to death. It spins just right so we neither fall off nor feel dizzy because it spins at the same rate as our ability to function within the force of gravity. How could that happen? Our God is glorious. That's how it happens. We have a glorious God.

God's passion is for His glory, that there be a visible recognition that He alone is God. His glory was visible to Israel at the tabernacle. Israel built a tabernacle that was not particularly exciting to look at on the outside. But after they built it, the glory of the Lord came in the "glory cloud." Exodus 40 tells us about it:

> Then the cloud covered the tent of meeting, and the glory of the LORD filled the tabernacle. And Moses was not able to enter the tent of meeting because the cloud had settled on it, and the glory of the LORD filled the tabernacle. Throughout all their journeys whenever the cloud was taken up from over the tabernacle, the sons of Israel would set out; but if the cloud was not taken up, then they did not set out until the day when it was taken up. For throughout all their journeys, the cloud of the LORD was on the tabernacle by day, and there was fire in it by night, in the sight of all the house of Israel. (vv. 34–38)

What a great passage. God came down and rested on the tabernacle as the glory cloud filled the Holy of Holies and all of the tabernacle. The reason God had to come in a cloud was because He had to veil His glory. He could not reveal His inner core, His full inner light. But the beauty of the glory cloud was that when the cloud moved, Israel moved. When the glory cloud stopped, Israel stopped. They would not budge until the cloud moved, and when it moved, they got up right away.

Here is a vital principle for Christian living. When you live your life for the glory of God, you do not have to worry about His will. The glory cloud leads you. When you follow the glory of God, when you have a passion for it, God's glory will always pick you up and pull you forward when it is time to move, then set you down and keep you still when it is time to stay. So do not look for God's will; look for His glory, and you will find His will.

Later, following the tabernacle, Israel built a permanent residence for the glory of God called the temple. At the temple's dedication, the glory cloud so filled the place that the priests could not do their work (1 Kings 8:10–11). God now had a permanent resting place for His presence among His people.

When God's presence was among His people, it meant His attributes were among His people. So they had the power of God, the knowledge of God, the presence of God, the truth of God, the revelation of God, the Spirit of God, the guidance of God, and anything else necessary because to have the glory of God is to have God, to have all His attributes at work for you.

Nothing is more important in life than the glory of God.

Conversely, when the people disobeyed God, the Bible says that over Israel was written "Ichabod," which means "The glory has departed from Israel" (1 Sam. 4:21). When the glory cloud leaves you, you are in trouble because you have no presence of God. You can pray, but you will not experience God's power. You can call out, but you will not experience God's presence.

But neither creation nor the tabernacle nor the temple was the ultimate revelation of God's glory in history, of course. God's visible glory was most fully seen in the person of Jesus Christ. John 1 puts it this way:

> In the beginning was the Word, and the Word was with God, and the Word was God. . . . And the Word became flesh, and dwelt among us, and we saw His glory, glory as of the only begotten from the Father, full of grace and truth. . . . No one has seen God at any time; the only begotten God [Jesus], who is in the bosom of the Father, He has explained [revealed] Him. (vv. 1, 14, 18)

In His earthly life, Jesus Christ was God's glory in human flesh. That's why He did what only God could do: heal the blind and the sick, raise the dead, read people's minds, and know what was happening ahead of time. Jesus was the visible manifestation of God in human flesh. His glory was veiled, though, because no one can look on God and live.

But in Matthew 17, Jesus took Peter, James, and John up to a mountain. There Christ zipped down His humanity, so to speak. He took off the veil of flesh for just a minute, and the Bible says that bursting out of His humanity was a bright light. And the voice from heaven was so awesome they had to hide their faces because the glory of God was on the mountain (vv. 1–8). Jesus Christ is God incarnate, the magnificent revelation of God in terms human beings can understand because He was God become Man.

God has not only manifested His glory in nature, in the tabernacle, in the temple, and in Christ. God's glory is also manifested in the church:

> Now to Him who is able to do far more abundantly beyond all that we ask or think, according to the power that works within us, to Him be the glory in the church. (Eph. 3:20–21)

Not only is there to be glory in the Son of God; there is to be glory through the people of God. We should reflect the attributes of God in our world. The church is designed to be a unique gathering of God's people through whom God mirrors His glory. This world should see our glorious God when they see the functioning of His people.

Only then will the church see that He is "able to do far more abundantly beyond all that we ask or think." In fact, that is true not only at the collective level, but also are the individual level because Ephesians 1:12 says that God saved you that you might live "to the praise of His glory." As we saw earlier, He wants your life to glorify Him.

OUR RESPONSE TO GOD'S GLORY

Only two groups of beings will not voluntarily glorify God: fallen humans and fallen angels. Both will be discarded from His presence because throughout all eternity, God will only fellowship with those who voluntarily bring Him glory.

Your claim to esteem God will be validated by how you respond to the God you say you esteem. The proof that you glorify God, that you recognize His intrinsic value, will be the value that you ascribe to His glory.

We parents often have trouble teaching our children how to handle money. We spend a lot of time trying to teach them the value of money because we want them to handle it wisely. Of course, kids will always say, "I got it. I know how to handle money. I've learned how to value it."

But the test is not having your kids tell you they value money. The test is how they spend it. How much money do they squander? The proof of how much we value God's glory is how we respond to it. How should we respond to God's glory? Psalm 96 gives us some great answers:

Sing to the LORD a new song;
Sing to the LORD, all the earth.
Sing to the LORD, bless His name;
Proclaim good tidings of His salvation from day to day.
Tell of His glory among the nations. (vv. 1–3)

One of my favorite songs some years ago was by the Winans.
They sang, "Everything you touch is a song."[7] Many of us do not
know that when cows moo, they are giving glory to God. When
kittens meow, they give glory to God. Dogs bark to the glory
of God. When the rooster wakes up and crows, he is saying,
"Cock-a-doodle-do, God!" We do not understand that when the
lion roars, he is giving glory to God.

You say, "Wait a minute! I don't believe those things are giving glory to God." Look at verses 11–13 of this psalm:

Let the heavens be glad, and let the earth rejoice;
Let the sea roar, and all it contains.
Let the field exult, and all that is in it.
Then all the trees of the forest will sing for joy
Before the LORD, for He is coming.

If everything on earth shouts God's glory, what should we
be doing? Go back to verses 7–9:

Ascribe to the LORD, O families of the peoples,
Ascribe to the LORD glory and strength.
Ascribe to the LORD the glory of His name;
Bring an offering and come into His courts.
Worship the LORD in holy attire.

7, The Winans, "Everything You Touch Is a Song" (1984).

Even your clothing ought to be whistling the glory of God. "Tremble before Him, all the earth" (v. 9). That is what people do who glorify God. They do not come and mumble little words. Even if they cannot sing, they break out in song because the ability to make a joyful noise was given by God.

Many people do not even give God what the animals give Him. Because we cannot interpret all those sounds, we think they are just a lot of noise. No, the Bible says that all of creation resonates with the glory of God, except people. God demands and deserves glory. We cannot give Him glory, because He already has it. It is intrinsic to him. We ascribe to Him the glory that He is due.

A judge becomes glorious when he puts on his robe. But when he takes off the robe, he is just another man. A police officer is glorious when she has on a badge and a blue uniform, but take off the badge and the uniform, and she is just another person. God is always glorious because He never takes off His "uniform." He never takes off His robe of glory. He is the King of the universe. He is glorious.

How much should we do this thing called glorifying God? Psalm 113:3–4 puts it this way: "From the rising of the sun to its setting the name of the Lord is to be praised. The LORD is high above all nations; His glory is above the heavens." When you open your eyes in the morning, praise Him. When you go into the bathroom and look in the mirror, praise Him. When you go to the breakfast table, praise Him. When you get in your car, praise Him. When He takes you safely to work, praise Him.

For the fact that you have work to go to and He gives you a mind to understand it, praise Him. When the day ends and you are still alive to go back home, praise Him. When you get home and have dinner, praise Him. When you see the rest of your family that He brought safely home, praise Him. When you retire for the night, praise Him. The Bible says the Lord is enthroned on the praises of His people (Ps. 22:3).

One day, Jesus came upon ten lepers who cried out, "have mercy on us!" (Luke 17:13). The Lord had pity on them and said, "Go and show yourselves to the priests" (v. 14). As they went, their skin became like babies' skin. The leprosy was gone.

> Nine of the lepers kept going, but one—a foreigner, a Samaritan—turned around, came back, fell on his knees before Jesus, and glorified Him. Jesus looked at him and said, "Were there not ten cleansed? But the nine—where are they?" (v. 17)

He asked a great question. Where are all the people to whom God has given life, health, and strength? How can we stay in bed on Sunday morning when God has given us strength? How can we be too tired for Him when, if it were not for Him, we would not be here at all? How can we not give Him glory? He deserves glory, not excuses.

God deserves our giving of His glory through all we pursue, not only in terms of our worship but by what we do each day. The Bible contains many examples:

1. God is glorified when we "bear much fruit" (John 15:8).
2. God is glorified when we do good works—apply biblical truths to human situations (Matt. 5:16).
3. God is glorified by our sexual purity (1 Cor. 6:18–20).

4. God is glorified when we confess our sins (Josh. 7:19).

5. God is glorified when we live by faith and not by sight (Rom. 4:19–21).

6. God is glorified when we proclaim His Word (2 Thess. 3:1).

7. God is glorified when we appeal to His glory in our suffering (1 Peter 4:14–16).

8. God is glorified when we do His will (John 17:4).

9. God is glorified when we confess His Son (Phil. 2:10).

10. God is glorified when we reflect the character of Christ (Rom. 15:6).

God has given us so many ways to give Him glory. He created the world so glory is due Him. Yet even when unbelievers do not voluntarily glorify God, God still gets what He wants—glory to Himself—even out of them. Remember what Pharaoh said to Moses in Egypt? "I'm not going to let you and your people go."

However, God told Moses, "Don't worry about Pharaoh. His heart is hard. I'm going to make it harder. I'm going to make him so mad at Me that he will do exactly what I want him to do. I will harden Pharaoh's heart and still get glory from him" (see Ex. 14:17).

It is not only Pharaoh's heart God has hardened. As we see in Romans 1:21, those who do not give Him glory run into a similar consequence. It says, "For although they knew God, they neither glorified him as God nor gave thanks to him, but their thinking became futile and their foolish hearts were darkened" (NIV).

Jeremiah 13:15–16 puts the warning against failure to give God glory this way,

> Hear and pay attention,
>> do not be arrogant,
>> for the LORD has spoken.
> Give glory to the LORD your God
>> before he brings the darkness,
> before your feet stumble
>> on the darkening hills.
> You hope for light,
>> but he will turn it to utter darkness
>> and change it to deep gloom.

Revelation 14:6–7 states,

> Then I saw another angel flying in midair, and he had the eternal gospel to proclaim to those who live on the earth—to every nation, tribe, language and people. He said in a loud voice, "Fear God and give him glory, because the hour of his judgment has come. Worship him who made the heavens, the earth, the sea and the springs of water."

So the issue is really not whether we will give God glory. If someone chooses not to give God glory on earth, they will do so eventually. The issue is more about when. Whether we give it to Him voluntarily or He has to squeeze it out of us against our wills, we are going to give God glory. God will get glory.

But given the fact of all that He's done for us, does not

He deserve it? Should not we be hurrying to give Him glory? Giving God glory not only pleases Him but it also strengthens and transforms us. Second Corinthians 3:18 is another beautiful passage of Scripture on the critical nature of God's glory. Paul writes:

> But we all, with unveiled face, beholding as in a mirror the glory of the Lord, are being transformed into the same image from glory to glory, just as from the Lord, the Spirit.

If you ever catch hold of this principle of the glory of the Lord, you will be transformed. Do you want to transform yourself? Do you have things in your life that need to be changed? Catch hold of the glory of God. Do you want to see your mate change? Don't nag him or her. Point the person to the glory of God.

To understand what Paul's talking about, we need to go back to verse 13: "Moses . . . used to put a veil over his face so that the sons of Israel would not look intently at the end of what was fading away." Paul is referring to an incident in Exodus 34, which continues the text discussed at the opening of this chapter.

On that mountain, Moses saw the glory of God—actually, he saw God's back because that's all he could take. Then as Moses came down the mountain, his face started to shine because he had been in God's presence. But the farther he went, the more the shine started to fade. By the time he got to the people, he had only a little shine left. Moses covered his face so the people would not see his shine fading. When he needed a new amount, he would have to march right back to the mountain to get a new shine. But when he came down to the people, his shine began to fade.

We are sort of like that. When we walk out of church on Sunday morning, most of us are shining because we have been in God's presence and have seen His glory. But by the time we get home and sit down around the table for lunch, we have lost some, or most, of our shine, which is the manifestation of His presence.

When my children were younger, I used to take them to amusement parks. Whenever we went, they always had those long green strings that glowed in the dark. Maybe you remember them.

My kids always wanted one, of course, so I would buy one for each of them, and they would wrap those strings around their necks or wrists and watch them glow. When we got in the car to go home, the kids wanted all the lights out so they could watch their strings glow. When we got home, they would go in their rooms and turn off the lights to watch the glow.

But after about an hour at home, the "glory" in those strings began to fade. The glow began to get dim. By the time the kids woke up the next day, the strings did not glow at all. The salesman does not tell you when you pay a small fortune for those strings that they have no light in them at all. They are not glowing because they have light in themselves. They glow only because of their exposure to light.

The moment a person removes that string from the light, it progressively loses its ability to glow because it is no longer exposed to the thing that made it glow in the first place: the light. To make it glow again, you need only to wrap it around a light bulb and let the light infiltrate the covering. In other words, simply expose it to that which gives it the ability to glow.

When Jesus Christ saved you, He put a new covering on you so that when you live in light of the glory of God, it will put a glow in your life. But when you remove yourself from God's glory, your glow begins to diminish. When you find that happening, you need to wrap yourself around the light of God's glory. Then the transforming work of God can begin to glow in you again.

David said that when he made the Lord the priority of his life, he had great gladness and joy (Ps. 16:8–9). The way he got joy was not by looking for it. He exposed himself to the glory of God. If you get exposed to His glory, the light begins to shine; change begins to take place; you have power you did not have before; you have victory you did not have before. Why? Not because of you, but because of the glory of God. It transforms you from within.

If you will just remember to thank and glorify God every time you do anything from now on, you will begin to shine, and the glory cloud will transform your life. If you want to be transformed, submit to passionately pursuing God's glory. If you want to tap into supernatural power, reflect God's glory. If you want to fulfill your life's purpose, bask in and radiate God's glory. Stop seeking to share it. Let God be God, and let the light of His glory shine through you. Paul makes this truth absolutely clear in 2 Corinthians 3:17–18. In this passage, Paul teaches that when the Word of God (mirror) is connected with the Spirit of God, we will be transformed. This transformation takes us from one level of glory to another as Christ's growing light in our lives progressively radiates God's glory in and through us.

Appendix

THE URBAN ALTERNATIVE

The Urban Alternative (TUA) equips, empowers, and unites Christians to impact *individuals, families, churches,* and *communities* through a thoroughly kingdom agenda worldview. In teaching truth, we seek to transform lives.

The core cause of the problems we face in our personal lives, homes, churches, and societies is a spiritual one; therefore, the only way to address it is spiritually. We've tried a political, social, economic, and even a religious agenda.

It's time for a **Kingdom agenda**.

The Kingdom agenda can be defined as the visible manifestation of the comprehensive rule of God over every area of life.

The unifying central theme throughout the Bible is the glory of God and the advancement of His kingdom. The conjoining thread from Genesis to Revelation—from beginning to end—is focused on one thing: God's glory through advancing God's kingdom.

When you do not have that theme, the Bible becomes disconnected stories that are great for inspiration but seem to be unrelated in purpose and direction. The Bible exists to share God's movement in history toward the establishment and expansion of His kingdom highlighting the connectivity throughout which is the kingdom. Understanding that increases the relevancy of this several thousand-year-old manuscript to your day-to-day living, because the kingdom is not only then, it is now.

The absence of the kingdom's influence in our personal and family lives, churches, and communities has led to a deterioration in our world of immense proportions:

- People live segmented, compartmentalized lives because they lack God's kingdom worldview.
- Families disintegrate because they exist for their own satisfaction rather than for the kingdom.
- Churches are limited in the scope of their impact because they fail to comprehend that the goal of the church is not the church itself, but the kingdom.
- Communities have nowhere to turn to find real solutions for real people who have real problems because the church has become divided, ingrown, and unable to transform the cultural landscape in any relevant way.

The kingdom agenda offers us a way to see and live life with a solid hope by optimizing the solutions of heaven. When God, and His rule, is no longer the final and authoritative standard under which all else falls, order and hope leaves with Him. But the reverse of that is true as well: As long as you have God, you have hope. If God is still in the picture, and as long as His agenda is still on the table, it's not over.

Even if relationships collapse, God will sustain you. Even if finances dwindle, God will keep you. Even if dreams die, God will revive you. As long as God, and His rule, is still the overarching rule in your life, family, church, and community, there is always hope.

Our world needs the King's agenda. Our churches need the King's agenda. Our families need the King's agenda.

In many major cities, there is a loop that drivers can take when they want to get somewhere on the other side of the city, but don't necessarily want to head straight through downtown. This loop will take you close enough to the city so that you can see its towering buildings and skyline, but not close enough to actually experience it.

This is precisely what we, as a culture, have done with God. We have put Him on the "loop" of our personal, family, church, and community lives. He's close enough to be at hand should we need Him in an emergency, but far enough away that He can't be the center of who we are.

We want God on the "loop," not the King of the Bible who comes downtown into the very heart of our ways. Leaving God on the "loop" brings about dire consequences as we have seen in our own lives and with others. But when we make God, and His rule, the centerpiece of all we think, do, or say, it is then that we will experience Him in the way He longs to be experienced by us.

He wants us to be kingdom people with kingdom minds set on fulfilling His kingdom's purposes. He wants us to pray, as Jesus did, "not My will, but Yours be done" (Luke 22:42). Because His is the kingdom, the power, and the glory.

There is only one God, and we are not Him. As King and Creator, God calls the shots. It is only when we align ourselves underneath His comprehensive hand that we will access His full power and authority in all spheres of life: personal, familial, church, and community.

As we learn how to govern ourselves under God, we then transform the institutions of family, church, and society from a biblically based kingdom worldview.

Under Him, we touch heaven and change earth.

To achieve our goal, we use a variety of strategies, approaches, and resources for reaching and equipping as many people as possible.

BROADCAST MEDIA

Millions of individuals experience *The Alternative with Dr. Tony Evans* through the daily radio broadcast playing on nearly **1,400 radio outlets** and in over **130 countries**. The broadcast can also be seen on several television networks and is viewable online at TonyEvans.org. You can also listen or view the daily broadcast by downloading the Tony Evans app for free in the app store. Over 18,000,000 message downloads/streams occur each year.

LEADERSHIP TRAINING

The Tony Evans Training Center (TETC) facilitates educational programming that embodies the ministry philosophy of Dr. Tony Evans as expressed through the kingdom agenda. The training courses focus on leadership development and discipleship in the following five tracks:

- Bible and Theology
- Personal Growth
- Family and Relationships
- Church Health and Leadership Development
- Society and Community Impact Strategies

The TETC program includes courses for both local and online students. Furthermore, TETC programming includes course work for non-student attendees. Pastors, Christian leaders, and Christian laity, both local and at a distance, can seek out The Kingdom Agenda Certificate for personal, spiritual, and professional development. For more information, visit: tonyevanstraining.org

The Kingdom Agenda Pastors (KAP) provides a *viable network* for *like-minded pastors* who embrace the Kingdom Agenda philosophy. Pastors have the opportunity to go deeper with Dr. Tony Evans as they are given greater biblical knowledge, practical applications, and resources to impact individuals, families, churches, and communities. KAP welcomes *senior and associate pastors* of all churches. KAP also offers an annual summit held each year in Dallas with intensive seminars, workshops, and resources.

Pastors' Wives Ministry, founded by Dr. Lois Evans, provides *counsel, encouragement,* and *spiritual resources* for pastors' wives as they serve with their husbands in the ministry. A primary focus of the ministry is the KAP Summit that offers senior pastors' wives a safe place to *reflect, renew,* and *relax* along with training in personal development, spiritual growth, and care for their emotional and physical well-being.

COMMUNITY & CULTURAL INFLUENCE

National Church Adopt-A-School Initiative (NCAASI) prepares churches across the country to impact communities by using *public schools as the primary vehicle for effecting positive social change* in urban youth and families. Leaders of churches, school districts, faith-based organizations, and other nonprofit organizations are equipped with the knowledge and tools to *forge partnerships* and build *strong social service delivery systems.* This training is based on the comprehensive church-based community impact strategy conducted by Oak Cliff Bible Fellowship. It addresses such areas as economic development, education, housing, health revitalization, family renewal, and racial reconciliation. We assist churches in tailoring the model to meet specific needs of their communities while simultaneously addressing the spiritual and moral frame of reference. Training events are held annually in the Dallas area at Oak Cliff Bible Fellowship.

Athlete's Impact (AI) exists as an outreach both into and through the sports arena. Coaches are the most influential factor in young people's lives, even ahead of their parents. With the growing rise of fatherlessness in our culture, more young people are looking to their coaches for guidance, character development, practical needs, and hope. After coaches on the influencer scale fall athletes. Athletes (whether professional or amateur) influence younger athletes and kids within their spheres of impact. Knowing this, we have made it our aim to equip and train coaches and athletes on how to live out and utilize their God-given roles for the benefit of the kingdom. We aim to do this through our iCoach app as well as resources such as *The Playbook: A Life Strategy Guide for Athletes.*

Tony Evans Films ushers in positive life change through compelling video-shorts, animation, and feature-length films. We seek to build kingdom disciples through the power of story. We use a variety of platforms for viewer consumption and have over 35,000,000 digital views. We also merge video shorts and film with relevant Bible study materials to bring people to the saving knowledge of Jesus Christ and to strengthen the body of Christ worldwide. Tony Evans Films released its first feature-length film, *Kingdom Men Rising*, in April 2019, in over eight hundred theaters nationwide, in partnership with Lifeway Films.

RESOURCE DEVELOPMENT

We are fostering lifelong learning partnerships with the people we serve by providing a variety of published materials. Dr. Evans has published more than one hundred unique titles based on over forty years of preaching whether that is in booklet, book, or Bible study format. He also holds the honor of writing and publishing the first full-Bible commentary and study Bible by an African American, released in 2019.

For more information, and a complimentary copy of
Dr. Evans's devotional newsletter,
call (800) 800-3222
or write TUA at P.O. Box 4000, Dallas TX 75208,
or visit us online

www.TonyEvans.org

ACKNOWLEDGMENTS

I want to thank my friends at Moody Publishers for their long-standing partnership in bringing my thoughts, study, and words to print. I particularly want to thank Greg Thornton for his friendship over the years, as well as his pursuit of excellence in all he does, and Kevin Emmert, Erik Peterson, and Connor Sterchi for their help in the process. In addition, my appreciation goes out to Heather Hair for her skills and insights in collaboration on this manuscript.

MORE FROM TONY EVANS

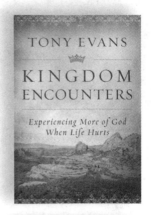

What all Christians need is a kingdom encounter. In *Kingdom Encounters*, Tony Evans explores how the faithful characters of Scripture encountered God—and were forever changed. Join Dr. Evans as he explores how these moments bolster your faith, restore your hope, and make clear to you the face of God.

978-0-8024-1925-5

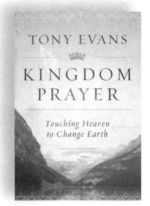

There is much God won't do in a Christian's life apart from prayer. In this practical overview, Tony Evans covers a variety of topics about prayer, including its principles, power, and purposes. He will help you see prayer's critical importance and encourage you to make it a dominant mark of your life.

978-0-8024-1484-7

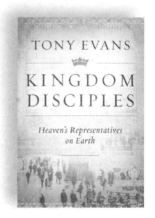

In *Kingdom Disciples*, Tony Evans outlines a simple, actionable definition of discipleship to help the church fulfill its calling. Readers will learn what a disciple is and cares about, how to be and make disciples, and what impact true discipleship has on the community and world.

978-0-8024-1203-4

also available as eBooks

MOODY
Publishers*

*From the Word to Life**